Notes and Memories of Cambodia

BY

B. Marrot

Officer of the Royal Order of Cambodia
1885
Gold medal (Cambodia's highest order)
bestowed by King Norodom
1899

Original monograph by B. Marrot
translated into English from the French
by
Marie-Helene Arnauld

Introduction, Notes, Commentary
and additional images
by
Joel Montague

Published by Datasia Press
2019
www.datasia.us

© Copyright, Original Translation, Text and Design, 2019:
Marie-Hélène Arnauld and Joel Montague.

Photo Restoration by Artsiom Yatsevich

IBSN: 978-1-934431-23-8

Front Cover Photo: North Gate of Angkor Thom
Jim Mizerski, 2011

TABLE OF CONTENTS

INTRODUCTION v
- THE EXPOSITION OF LYON IN 1894 v
- THE BOOK PRINTED BY BERNARD MARROT
  AT THE LYON EXPOSITION vii
- CAMBODIA DURING THE YEARS
  WHEN MARROT LIVED THERE xii
- MARROT, THE BUSINESS MAN IN CAMBODIA xv

NOTES AND MEMORIES OF CAMBODIA 1

OVERVIEW 1
- CAMBODIA – ITS HISTORY 2
- THE SECOND KING - MANDARINS 10
- FREE MEN - SLAVES - SAVAGES 11
- RELIGION - BUDDHISM 13
- PHNOM-PENH - THE MEKONG 18
- CAMBODIANS - HABITS - CUSTOMS 27
- CELEBRATIONS 37
- FISHING ON THE GREAT LAKE 43
- THE RUINS OF ANGKOR 46

PRODUCTS OF CAMBODIA 51
- TOBACCO 51
- PEPPER 51
- COFFEE 52
- THE MULBERRY TREE 52
- COTTON 52
- CARDAMOM 53
- IRON ORE 54
- TORTOISE SHELL 54
- DEPOSITS OF SALTPETER, LIME AND CLAY 56

OUR CURRENT SITUATION IN CAMBODIA IN 1894 57

ADDITIONAL PHOTOGRAPHS 61

BIBLIOGRAPHY 85

ACKNOWLEDGEMENTS 86

INTRODUCTION

THE EXPOSITION OF LYON IN 1894

The longish monograph, or rather short book, which follows, entitled (a translation from the French title), "Notes and Memories of Cambodia," is by Bernard Marrot, otherwise known as "Raoul" Marrot. It was originally a monograph which appeared at an obscure French "World's Fair" or, as the Francophone nations called it, "an international exposition" in the city of Lyon in 1894. Such grandiose events, now rare, were all the rage in Europe and the United States for much of the nineteenth and early twentieth centuries where countries competed to break records on attendance by the public. An acerbic description of the real objectives of such extravagant events was made by Florence Vidal where she, when describing the "Exposition universelle, internationale et coloniale," held in Lyon, wrote that the exposition was a typical example of an educational effort which had gone awry in order to please and entertain the public:

> Universal exhibitions, those grandiose events very useful in their time, have marked the collective memory. However, despite their edifying intentions, it is above all through their festive atmosphere, their fireworks and their colourful shows that they have marked peoples' minds. In principle, an exposition was not a festival. One went there to inform oneself, to learn. But then year after year, in those venues where one persisted in exhibiting stories about work and other sections of the social economy, typical French leisure activities, the fair-goers' curiosity grew and they ended up winning. To the economic, political and didactic problems which totally dominated the first expositions had progressively been added the desire, and even rather the necessity of entertainment in order to attract and keep the public interested. In 1894, the City, swarming with animation and multiple attractions of Lyon, had perfectly understood this. It is not enough for an exhibition to be big and beautiful, it also has to be swarming with animation, multiple attractions and constantly renewed liveliness.[1]

---

1 Translated from Florence Vidal, "Lyon 1894. La Fete S'invite: a L'EXPO," *Diplome national de master, Universite Lumiere*, Lyon 2, p. 173.

Some detail on the "Exposition universelle, internationale et coloniale" where Marrot's publication appeared is perhaps worth noting. The main building of the Exposition was an enormous structure with a 55-meter high dome measuring 242 meters across. There were dedicated pavilions at the Exposition covering education (Palais de l'enseignement), the city of Paris, the city of Lyon and its surroundings (Département du Rhône), Religion (Palais des arts religieux), Economy (Palais de l'économie sociale), as well as Art, Agriculture, Labour, Railways, Civil Engineering and Forestry Services.

Although the title of the Exposition included the word "colonial," its colonial element was really quite small for the French public had no great interest in being educated on the constituent territories of France's enormous colonial empire, second then only to the British in size.

The fact of the matter was the French public was totally disinterested in the French Empire and the great explorer Francis Garnier wrote in 1969 upon his return to France:

> One is struck by the public's profound indifference to all aspects of the Colonial contribution to our national greatness... There seems to be no connection between the overseas interests which one has just defended and that Metropolitan power which, sunk back on itself, does not even dream of seeking overseas outlets for the restless activity consuming it alone.[2]

The Exposition which is now somewhat obscure among the many, many colonial exhibitions in France in the late nineteenth and early twentieth centuries drew unwanted and unexpected attention with the assassination at the Exposition of the then-French president, Sadi Carnot, during his visit to Lyon on July 24, 1894. It seems likely that the assassination was unrelated

---

2   Francis Garnier, "Voyages d'exploration en Indochine," April 1869, quoted in C.M. Andrew and A. S. Kayna-Forstner, "Center and Periphery in the Making of the Second French Colonial Empire, 1815-1920," *Journal of Imperial and Commonwealth History* 16, no. 3 (1988).

to the so-called "Panama scandal" (1892) which occurred when the French press discovered that the Panama Canal Company had bribed French politicians in an effort to save the collapsing project. Rather, the president was stabbed by an angry Italian anarchist who was later tried and put to death. The Exposition with some trepidation stayed open after the assassination and did well. Three million eight hundred thousand people attended the Exposition.

THE BOOK PRINTED BY BERNARD MARROT AT THE LYON EXPOSITION

The monograph (which we have translated into English) which follows our introduction was originally entitled in French, "Notes et Souvenirs sur le Cambodge." Prior to being printed by the author, it was one of the many essays on French Indochina which appeared in a lengthy book published by the Lyon Chamber of Commerce in 1894.[3]

At the Exposition itself, there was a "Palais de l'Indo-Chine" (Indochina Palace) which included five sections, each of which had a showroom with cultural and commercial objects from Annam, Tonkin, Cochinchine, Cambodia and Laos. Besides having floor space with photographs, literature, arts and crafts and commercial products, each country was described in the book by an essay on that particular country. The section on Indochina

---

3   "Exposition coloniale organisee par la chamber de commerce a l'Exposition universelle de Lyon en 1894", *Pila Chambre de commerce et d'industrie*. The article entitled "Le Cambodge" runs from page 162 through page 192 and adds at the end the author is identified by the two initials "C.C." At the back of the book, under the heading of "Composition de l'adminstration et du personnel" under the subheading of "Palais de l'indochine," under IV "Cambodge" the text is "Commissiare M. B. Marrot, negociant a Phnom- Penh." On page 270, under the heading "Collaborateurs Medailles D'or," on page 271, Marrot (B.), Commissiare du Cambodge, was identified as receiving a gold medal.

opens with the text of a speech by the King of Annam which was made at the opening of the Indochina Pavilion. Bernard Marrot officially represented Cambodia at the Exposition and wrote the description of Cambodia for the book (see above) but he was obviously unhappy with the short shrift given to Cambodia in the book and at the Exhibition itself. Perhaps the reason was that Cambodia, as it appeared in the official Exposition book and in the Exposition itself was less important and less viable commercially than the other countries of Indochina. He thus released quite separately, privately printed and sold for 1 franc 50, the very monograph on Cambodia (translated into English) which is just a duplicate of the essay in the Chamber of Commerce book. However, in the Chamber of Commerce version he wrote:

> Of the four Indochinese exhibitions, the Cambodian exhibition was the one that presented itself under the brightest and richest aspect, and this was due to the magnificent art collections which the curator, Mr. Marrot, had displayed, also to the clever layout of all the products of the section. The display cabinet containing the coins and some samples of the kingdom's old silver and gold work was admired by all the visitors.
>
> The ethnographic collection which was comprised of about one hundred pieces intended for the Cambodian people had been thought about with much care; among those were some very old ones, dating back more than one thousand years, and which cannot be found in any other collection.
>
> The figures of divinities copied from those of the temples of Angkor and other pagodas, constituted an art collection with a rare value.
>
> The furniture section featured the interior of a mandarin from Cambodia. It was very much admired. The collection of imported objects was also very complete, and so was that of the country's gross products.
>
> We must also mention collections of old Khmer weapons, a collection of Cambodian silk manufactured for the

indigenous rich class, a magnificent collection of wood for cabinet making and magnifying glasses used for veneering, with an extraordinary dimension and beauty, and finally two huge pictures painted on canvas, featuring the ruins of Angkor and adorning the walls.

In short, Cambodia produced a first-class art exhibition and a commercial one representing, as accurately as one could have desired, the economic and industrial state of this country which is still on the threshold of a new life which civilisation has just given it.[4]

The book that follows is of unusual interest because it represents the viewpoint of a private French businessman who had lived in Cambodia for many decades during a less well-known period of Cambodian history, that is, just after the French made Cambodia a "Protectorate." There are of course a number of official and quasi-official accounts of Cambodia written during that same period covering its monarchy, geography, customs, agricultural products, etc. There are also a number of superficial accounts by tourists and others. However, there is only one "memoire" actually done by an individual, not in any way associated with or in favor with the French Government, which provides esiderable detail on the country and the many changes made by the French. The book is even more unusual in that, unlike most of the other turgid material then available, it includes a number of original sketches and actual early photographs made during that same period. Marrot's short book provides a thoughtful commentary on the King and the Royal Palace, the ethnography and customs of Cambodia, the intricacies of Buddhism, a lengthy commentary on slavery and a host of other subjects. While he demonstrates a wry sense of humor when describing some of the Cambodian customs, his commentary is that of a man who was intensely interested in Cambodia and (like many of his more learned colleagues) totally overwhelmed by the beauty of Angkor Wat. In its reading, the monograph describes the extraordinary

---

4   Ibid. pp. 191-192.

change that took place after the capital was moved to Phnom Penh in Cambodia and describes a city almost totally changed and improved by the 1890s. Although he was almost grotesquely a self-centered individual, the author only mentions himself as a participant in the change on one occasion. He never mentions (quite odd indeed) other members of the French private sector in Cambodia who were attempting to do the same sort of thing as he was doing – that is, making money. Marrot himself was a member of an obscure group of individuals working in the private sector who were intensely disliked by the French government and the French military in Cambodia. They too, private citizens, had connections with the King.

The 30 photographs and sketches in the original book which are hereafter reproduced are of extremely varied quality but some are excellent. Many, however, such as the King's first wife (page 7), the Cambodian bonzes (page 7) and the coins and plates (pages 14 and 15) are hardly worth reproducing though we have done so as they were in the original book. That notwithstanding, it turns out that there are a large number of picture postcards which surfaced at the turn of the century in Phnom Penh taken by another businessman who lived there and who was no doubt a colleague of Marrot. Almost none of these (extremely rare) picture postcards have been published elsewhere though a few can be found in <u>Picture Postcards of Cambodia: 1900-1950</u> by one of the authors. That amateur photographer was, like Marrot, a businessman.. The photographer's name was Scipion Leblanc who apparently arrived in Phnom Penh in 1873. The photographs by Leblanc were in two series and Leblanc's name appears on the left-hand side (Edon S. Leblanc – PNOMPENH). The photographs are a worthy and virtually unknown addition to our understanding of what Phnom Penh looked during the same years when Marrot was working in the Protectorate. Though it is conjecture, we assume that Leblanc was still active after Marrot left. Nonetheless, we have thus added them and a few others of considerable rarity to this the book by Marrot as an appendix for they nicely compliment the photographs and images in the original book which was available at the Exposition in 1894.

According to an authority on early Cambodian photography, Jim Mizerski,[5] Leblanc is not listed in the 1894 "Annuaire du Cambodge" but in the 1901 "Annuaire général de l'Indo-Chine française" he was listed as a Phnom Penh merchant selling photographic products. Mizerski notes he may have been an amateur photographer or maybe just someone who marketed photographs taken by others such as Raquez.

Mizerski notes that a number of the photographs (mentioned above) were taken by Emile Gsell . A local business man (Roustan) may have been involved in adding the photographs actually taken by Gsell but Roustan implied that he may have taken them himself.[6]

At the very end of our work, we added a few additional, very early postcards which are unattributed, each of which, however, compliments the images in the book.

---

[5] Jim Mizerski, Personal correspondence, December 30, 2016.
[6] Jim Mizerski, Personal correspondence, October 12, 2016.

CAMBODIA DURING THE YEARS WHEN MARROT LIVED THERE

During the decades Marrot worked in Cambodia, Norodom ruled as King from 1860-1904. On June 17, 1884 the French authorities had forced the King to sign a treaty with France which consolidated the French position in Cambodia. The French moved the capital of their new "Protectorate" from the town of Oudong, where the Queen Mother lived, to Phnom Penh in 1866 and gradually the tiny city of Phnom Penh, where Marrot lived, was totally transformed in the following 30 years. Indeed, by the turn of the twentieth century, it was one of the most modern cities in Indochina.

A description of the Cambodian King while Marrot was living in Phnom Penh is as follows.

Osborne states:

> We have many descriptions of Norodom. We know that he was a small man, barely 5' tall with pock-marked skin. In the early years of his relations with the French, he appears to have readily adopted a style of dress modeled on European military fashion with tunics draped in gold lace. He liked western alcohol... and he was an opium smoker.[7]

The best description (translated from the French) of Phnom Penh in its early days is contained in a book published by the French Government shortly after Marrot departed which described the capital as follows:

> The capital is divided into three very different parts:
>
> 1. The so-called "European town" where the various departments of the Administration are established, most of the shops and the residences of the French community;
>
> 2. The so-called "Chinese town"; and
>
> 3. The "Cambodian district" occupied by the King's

---

7   *Phnom Penh: A Cultural History*. Milton Osborne, 2008, Oxford University Press, New York, p 66.

palace and its outbuildings. The town comprises few interesting buildings, however, some beautiful edifices adorn the main streets; notably: the mansion of the Resident Superior, the Town Hall, the Treasury, the large building of Customs and Excise, the Post and Telegraph, the Hospital, the infantry barracks, the Cathedral, the Grand Hotel, the offices of the Cabinet of Ministers and the Cambodian Courts. The style of some of these buildings recalls old Khmer architecture.

The King's palace is composed of a certain number of buildings built in the European style but with some Khmer adornments. The vast rectangle occupied by these constructions is surrounded by a crenellated wall, each side measuring 600 metres. A sumptuous pagoda has just been built within this wall by King Norodom. Among other precious objects, it contains a Buddha made of emerald; finally, a few rather interesting Cambodian and Chinese pagodas are scattered in the various districts.

The palace of the Second King is located in the "European" part of the town. An inner canal separates the European and the Chinese town. The outer canal, lined by an embankment which was turned into a beautiful avenue, encircles the whole city. This promenade planted with beautiful trees is very busy at certain times of the day. Six bridges, two of them being rather remarkable because of their size, were built over these canals at the busiest crossing points. The parapet of the bridge situated near the Treasury is a plaster cast of enormous "naga" (snakes with seven heads), the stone original versions of which can be found in the ruins of Angkor.

The town is lit by electricity and a plant equipped with huge filters supplies it with drinking water. A sewage system is being studied at the moment and will complete the improvement of the drainage of the capital and will make it a most pleasant town to live in.

There is a plan for the construction of embankments and their construction will satisfy the interest of trade.

The suburbs of the capital which are located beyond the outer canal form four big villages inhabited essentially by indigenous people.

They are: in the north, the Catholic village of Rossey Keo with the cathedral; in the south, the village of Takeo with the slaughter houses; in the east and on the other side of the Tonle-Sap, the very important village of Chrui-Changva with the water and electricity plant; a Catholic mission settled there as well. At the furthest point of the island of Chrui-Changva, there is an abandoned lighthouse. Finally, and lastly, in the west, the village of Bac-Tuc on the side of the road to Kampot. The town (Phnom Penh) comprises four very popular covered indoor markets, the biggest and the richest being the Central market located near the inner canal, at the junction of Quai Piquet and Rue Ohier.

The population of Phnom-Penh is about 60,000 inhabitants; it is quite mixed. In addition to Cambodian nationals, one finds Annamese, Chinese from all the provinces of the Celestial Empire, Malays, Indians, Filipinos (people from Manila), etc... There are about 400 Europeans. The population living on the water is considerable; it would be difficult to determine how many they are. They live mainly on junks and sampans berthed along the banks.

Phnom-Penh is the home port of more than fifty launches which daily serve numerous posts in Cambodia, Indochina, lower Laos and Siam, carrying passengers and goods and also towing junks, the removing of which is frequent at certain times of year.

The liners of the Compagnie des Messageries Fluviales operate the various postal services. During the high tides' season, a weekly service operates in Phnom-Penh and in Battambang and serves Siem Reap (ruins of Angkor). The traffic of the port is extremely busy. On many occasions the Chamber of Commerce expressed the wish to create a free port. During the high tides the largest ships can sail up the river all the way to Phnom-Penh. A mixed Advisory Chamber of Commerce and Agriculture was established by order of 30 April 1897; it is composed of settlers, traders or elected farmers and one indigenous member designated by the Administration.[8]

---

8   A translation of French Government, *Annuaire Illustre du Cambodge, 1904*, Claude et Cie Librairies Editeur, Saigon p. 123-127

MARROT, THE BUSINESS MAN IN CAMBODIA

Marrot, the businessman, lived and worked in the Phnom Penh described above from the early years of the French Protectorate to his departure at the end of the nineteenth century.

The early years of the life of Marrot are a bit hazy. Nonetheless, Greg Muller in his extraordinary book *Colonial Cambodia's 'Bad Frenchmen*[9], provides some background on him. He was born in France in 1855 and his mother "Madame Marrot" moved from Vietnam where they lived to Cambodia where she built up a prosperous business supplying the King, at that time King Norodom, with Parisian goods. The move took place in 1875 and it seems likely that Bernard Marrot returned to France somewhat less than 20 years later but remained very much in touch with Cambodia later in life. Madame Marrot was, at the time when she arrived, Phnom Penh's only white business woman and while her son's name was actually Raoul, he was called Bernard. There is no record of his schooling (in what is now Vietnam) which was possibly quite limited as the French of his monograph which follows was in some places exceedingly difficult to translate into English – but we have done our best.

Unlike a good many other European somewhat shady business people working in Cambodia (such as "Caraman," so vividly described by Muller), Bernard Marrot was quite successful and dealt frequently with the King. Muller estimates that in the early years of the Protectorate there were approximately 34 entrepreneurs and European traders seeking favor with the King and searching for investment opportunities.

The great scholar, Milton Osborne, writes that for the first two decades following the move of the capital to Phnom Penh, the city's existence revolved around two poles. "The first centered on Norodom and the Palace... the Palace was also a place

---

9   Muller, Gregor, *Colonial Cambodia's 'Bad Frechmen': The rise of French rule and the life of Thomas Caraman,* 1840-47, Routledge, 2006.

where the King was remarkably ready to deal with a motley cast of self-interested foreigners who were usually of dubious character and often out-and-out carpetbaggers."[10] The other pole described by Osborne "revolved around the French representative, whose official residence was cited close to the Phnom." Osborne notes[11] that "through the 1860s, 1870s and into the early 1880s, a pattern developed in which the French Representative pressed changes to the King's administration on the King..... Norodom would agree to implement them, he would then fail to act."

Describing the Court, Osborne notes:

> Wealthy Chinese were welcome as, perhaps most curiously, were the Europeans already briefly mentioned."[12] "French officialdom despised them but could not utterly ignore them because of their nationality. Norodom, on the other hand, was ready to meet them in a camaraderie that mixed joining them to play billiards – he had his own table – with using them as his agents to import goods from Europe and as a source of loans when he was temporarily short of funds. With readiness to flatter[13] him, he found them comforting relief from the often hectoring tone used by French officials when they dealt with him. "By 1897 the town of Phnom Penh had changed dramatically in terms of buildings but its population had risen to 50,000, of whom 400 were French, 22,000 were Chinese, 4,000 were Annamites and 16,000 were Cambodians. The squalid sodden village of the 1860s had been entirely changed by the turn of the century.
>
> Raoul Marrot was rewarded on a number of occasions by Royal decorations for his loyalty to the King by being made a "Chevalier" (1883) and then as Officer of the Royal Order (1885) and finally as recipient of the Medaille d'Or (1889). Muller notes, "that since in France, foreign honorary distinctions were generally subject to state control and

---

10   Ibid., <u>Osborne</u>, op. cit., p. 65.
11   Ibid., p. 65.
12   Muller, p. 197.
13   Ibid., p. 197,

prior authorizations, Marrot requested permission from the Chancellery for France's Légion d'Honneur, while in Paris in 1884-1885. The authorization was not granted. The reason appeared to be because his (Marrot's) actions were to the detriment of the French cause during the unrest of 1884 and 1885.[14] "In the perception of the colonial authorities, Marrot had forfeited his honor and was no longer entitled to lay claims to it by the public display of medals."

Marrot made a fortune in Cambodia, particularly in Phnom Penh. When he returned to France, he installed himself in Toulouse where he entered politics. He became an elected member of the Conseil Supérieur des Colonies as the delegate from Cambodia. He was then elected by the Parti Radical to the General Counsel of the Haute-Garonne in 1904. He was also assistant to the Mayor of Toulouse from 1898-1912. He left his chateau (the Chateau de Monlon, see photograph) and his lands to the Institut Agricole de l'Université de Toulouse.[15]

The justification for finally being awarded the French Legion of Honor noted that it was awarded because of his work as general counselor of the region of Haute-Garonne and deputy mayor of Toulouse with a public service of 22 years in "elective functions." He was said to have given help to various charity establishments and was president of numerous philanthropic associations. His work in Cambodia as a businessman is not mentioned in the awards documentation but it was said that he had carried out "missions abroad in the colonies, etc."

---

14   Ibid. p. 198.
15   Bernard Vouillot, Department de l'Orientation, Bibliographique nationale de France, 2015.

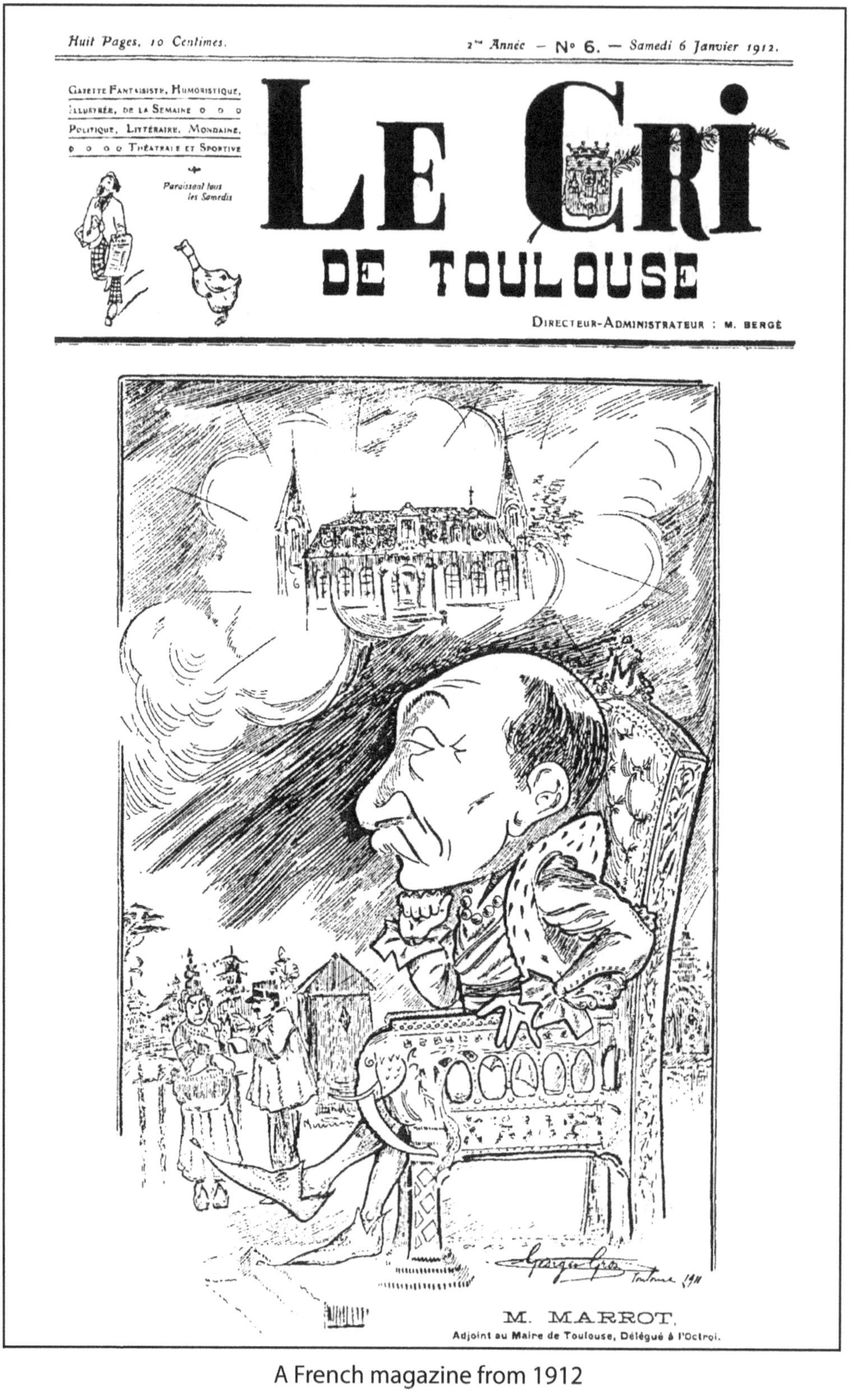

Huit Pages, 10 Centimes.

2me Année — N° 6. — Samedi 6 Janvier 1912.

Gazette Fantaisiste, Humoristique, Illustrée, de la Semaine, Politique, Littéraire, Mondaine, Théatrale et Sportive

Paraissant tous les Samedis

LE CRI DE TOULOUSE

Directeur-Administrateur : M. Bergé

M. MARROT,

Adjoint au Maire de Toulouse, Délégué à l'Octroi.

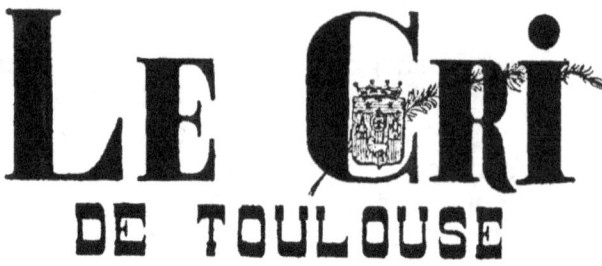

A French magazine from 1912

1. PALAIS DE L'ALGÉRIE - 2. PALAIS DE LA TUNISIE.
3. PALAIS DE L'ANNAM ET DU TONKIN.

Bulletin officiel de l'Exposition de Lyon:
Exposition de Lyon de 1894, 31 May 1894

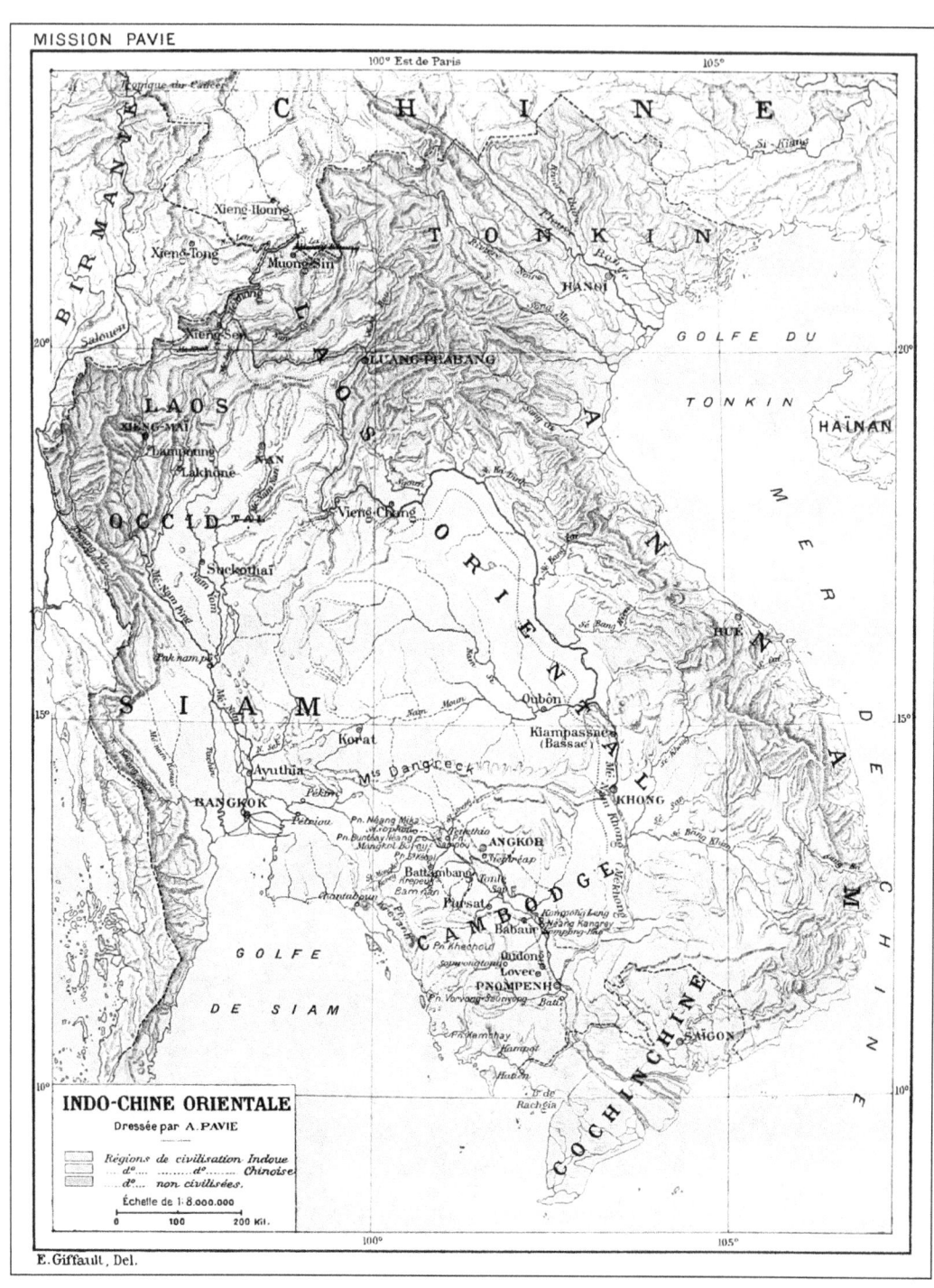

Map of Indochina including Cambodia
Mission Pavie Indo-Chine, 1879 - 1893. Etudes Diverses, I,
Paris, Ernest Leroux, Editeur, 19 Rue Bonaparte, 1898

Marrot's Chateau de Monlon

The Cambodian room of the Exposition of Lyon

Exposition de Lyon
1894
Section Cambodgienne

Notes et Souvenirs sur le Cambodge

avec de nombreuses gravures dans le texte

par B. MARROT

Officier de l'Ordre Royal du Cambodge
Délégué par le Protectorat Français
pour l'Organisation de l'Exposition Cambodgienne

PRIX : 1.50

GRANDE IMPRIMERIE FORÉZIENNE P. ROUSTAN_ROANNE.

NOTES AND MEMORIES OF CAMBODIA
OVERVIEW

CAMBODIA – ITS HISTORY

The kingdom of Cambodia, which strongly wished to occupy a place in the building (Palais de L'Indochine) erected recently by the city of Lyon in order to allow France to exhibit the variety of its industry, is still little known to Europeans. A few notes on this rich land, therefore, seemed indispensable to me to enlighten visitors who will hopefully call at the Cambodian section (of the Indochina building) for a few moments.

Just like the "happy Kings," the kingdom of Cambodia has virtually no well established history; in fact, one would, in order to find out the truth, go through a maze of the most fabulous legends. As for the accounts of the facts stated by the Chinese historians about Cambodia, one is allowed to ignore them, for most of the time they are a pack of lies and superstitions.

However, as we will see later when I write about the ruins of Angkor, when faced with remains of such gigantic and skillfully built monuments, one cannot but admit that Cambodia, in the past, must have been one of the most powerful empires of the peninsula of Indochina.

According to the partly destroyed documents remaining from that glorious era, it seems that Cambodia reached the height of its power around the 12th century. Invaded later by the Chinese it was continually perturbed by internecine wars with neighboring countries. This warfare is easily explained by the sole fact of its geographical position, that is to say, between the 10th and 13th degrees of latitude North and the 101st and 105th degree of longitude East. It is narrowly restricted in the north by Siam and in the south by Cochin-China, so that invaders found easy routes everywhere. The consequence was that it was sometimes a tributary of either Siam or Cochin-China, depending on how opportunities for invasion presented themselves. A certain Captain Savin de Larclauze[16] translated a letter written by a Cambodian which stated the facts as seen by the Cambodian at the begin-

---

16   [Captain Savin de Larclauze was the first French national married in Indochina. He married Ms. Domergue on February 11, 866. At that time, he was an inspector in Tay-Ninh. He was killed soon after in an ambush.]

ning of this century. The letter stated that this old Cambodian empire was in the past wealthy and fearsome. There only remained then (at the time of the letter) a small region ruined by external and civilian wars, and a tiny population dying under the oppression of its new masters.

The sovereign of Cambodia was thereafter (at that time) nothing but a fragile king watched by the Siamese and the Annamese, whose oppression paralyzed his will. This situation was so bad that the day France, after conquering Cochin-China, put Cambodia under its protection, it was a real day of celebration for its inhabitants who were then rid of the oppression of the Annamese.

KING NORODOM 1st

In August 1863, Cambodia, not being the enemy of Annam anymore, was freed from Siamese protection by a treaty which Admiral de La Grandiere (of France) signed with the current King, Norodom 1st. This was a treaty which placed Cambodia under a "Protectorate" of France. About a month later, in June 1864, Norodom 1st was solemnly crowned in Oudong, the old capital of the kingdom, in the palace of the King's mother. This celebration was carried out with all the usual ceremony: "the Queen Mother," the "Second King" and all the mandarins who had come from all over the kingdom and were dressed in their best bright colored silk clothes and by their presence asserted the supremacy of France vis-a-vis the new king.

[At the coronation] the King was crowned with the crown held in the hand of a high officer of the French navy and with the other hand being that of a Siamese ambassador. Commander Desmoulins delivered a very emphatic speech in order to celebrate the freedom of this kingdom which became an ally of France. At that time King Norodom 1st was twenty-eight years old. He (Norodom) is now fifty-eight and seems to want to live for many

King Norodom on His Throne

more years.

    I will spare the reader and not mention all the titles with which the King was attributed on his crowning. There are about twenty-five, all very pretentious, and they can be reduced to the following: Sâmdàch Prea Nôrôdom, Préachau Grung Campuchéa and Thup Bodey. They indicate that Norodom is the lord, celebrated by the powerful, that his feet and head are sacred, that he is descended from invisible spirits and that he is the master of souls, etc., etc.

    The King is small, rather thin and does not exercise much. He almost constantly stays in his palace and his great passion is smoking opium. Like all smokers of this narcotic it has become a

King Norodom

necessity in his life. He speaks Siamese and Cambodian which moreover he can write, but despite his long acquaintance with the French, he only knows the most commonly used words in our language. His face, open and very expressive, reveals a real happiness. It is with amiability that he welcomes the Europeans who visit him and he encourages them to come and live in Cambodia.

All the French traders who went to Cambodia did business with him, for he enjoys diversity in purchasing new products and by dealing with different companies, he is certain to learn about all the new products of which he is very fond.

The longest journey he ever made was the journey from Phnom-Penh to Manila. He often intended to visit France but he never undertook that vast project.

Usually (the King) wears the Cambodian costume and it is

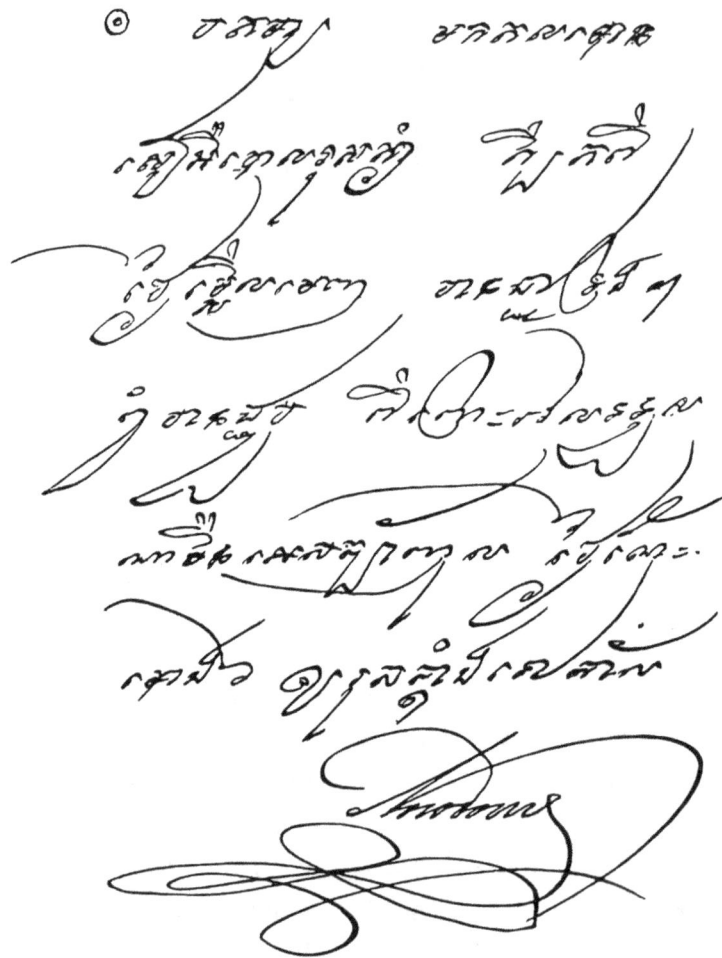

The King's Signature

only on days of celebrations or receptions that he wears a special outfit which is half Cambodian, half French, brightly covered with golden embroidery on the top of it. He wears the Grand Cross of the 'Legion of Honour', without forgetting the kepi of a Major General.

He has a very pronounced taste for all French-made articles such as furniture, curtains, wall covering, mirrors, silk, jewels, weapons, carriages, all of which are products kept in his palaces.

Since polygamy exists in Cambodia, the King is the one who practices it most unreservedly, for, generally speaking the number of wives corresponds to their master's wealth. The King has about one hundred wives in his establishment, but only a few are recognized as his real wives; the others are mainly dancers, singers or musicians who are supported in the palace so that they can perform on days of festivity in theatrical performances. They are watched by old women who play the role of eunuchs, those (eunuchs) having been eliminated a long time ago.

The King, when he is inside his palace, is always accompanied by about twenty women who are on duty in turn.

It would be difficult to say how many children they have exactly because he himself would get it wrong since he never kept a record of their birth certificates to check their births and later their deaths.

The King's First Wife

The eldest of his children, Machu Duong Chac (Yukanthor), to whom he gave all his affection, did not give him the satisfaction he felt he was entitled to expect. Brought up the European way, this prince who, right from birth, seemed uncommunicative, turned against his father once he reached adulthood. All his plans having been thwarted, he was sent to France where he continued to cause trouble through articles he had published in the Parisian newspapers. In order to put an end to this state of things, the French government had him arrested a few months ago and he was sent to Algeria where he is currently under custody.

I mentioned earlier, when enumerating the King's titles, that his head was sacred. Not only is no one allowed to touch it but it is also forbidden to put one's hand over it. To do so would be the biggest sacrilege, so much so that when he occupies a floor of his palace nobody is supposed to be on the floor above him. Nevertheless, since it is absolutely necessary to touch his head in order to cut his hair or to shave him, one solves the problem by performing a most important ceremony with the aim of purifying the hands of the barber to whom the remarkable honor has fallen. The ceremony is very pompous and is accompanied by music in the presence of the Bakus. These (the Bakus) are special priests descending from an old cast of Cambodians. They can get married, they have long hair, they wear a particular outfit and in turns they look after the Royal Sword which, thanks to them, was kept for several centuries. They mumble prayers which they don't understand, and since the assistants do not understand them either, it is probably why they are very respected and take part in all the ceremonies.

To finish on the subject of the respect due to the king, I will mention a custom which is not very well known by those who have never lived in Cambodia. For indigenous people, it consists in bowing and crawling on all fours every time they are in the presence of their king. As soon as he appears in the street, either on foot or in his carriage, immediately, along his entire route men, women and children alike bow, face to the ground, and wait until he is far away before raising their heads. The mandarins themselves are forced to follow the custom; they are allowed to talk to the King only if they bow at his feet without ever looking at him.

However, the King who is happily under the influence of our civilization, very often allows them not to perform these 'salamalecs'.

THE SECOND KING - MANDARINS

The second king, who has more or less as many titles as the first king, is given the name "Obbarack." He is the heir to the throne; he is the one who will replace Norodom when the latter dies, for a successor is never automatically appointed, but when in his turn he dies, the crown returns to Norodom's children.

The line of conduct of the "Obbarack" consists in doing on a small scale what the King does on a big scale for his resources do not allow him to have huge expenses. As a result, his power is nil.

I will say only a few words about the previous administration of the kingdom which was in the hands of Cambodian civil servants called "mandarins" because, since 1884, some major reforms modified that administration as we will see later.

Appointed and fired by the King, the mandarins do not receive a salary but they have a share in the customs revenues and in the fines generated by the courts.

There are ten levels in the hierarchy of the mandarins. All the ministers belong to the tenth level; there are ten ministries and only five have an "active" office. They have the most baroque names. Here I will explain the names in a more comprehensible language and in a hierarchical order. They are: the Minister of the Navy, the Minister of the Palace, the Minister of War, the Minister of Police, the Minister of Finance; then come the mandarins in charge of various services such as civil engineering, the care of the horses, the carriages, the elephants, etc.

Within the kingdom, each province has a Resident Governor, and under his command several subordinates and mayors of villages. All these mandarins gather twice a year in the King's palace for the ceremony of the "vow of faithfulness" which consists in drinking sacred water which has previously been prepared by the Bakus.

A ceremonial official recites the text of the vow; each mandarin repeats the words all through the reading of the text and then receives a little cup made of bronze from the hand of the Baku which contains the sacred water scooped out of big clay jugs. The sick mandarins must ask for the water to be delivered to their home; should they forget, they have to pay a fine.

FREE MEN - SLAVES - SAVAGES

The population of the kingdom, in addition to the mandarins, comprises free men and slaves and the monks forming the clergy. One must add straight away that the slaves are not slaves in our sense of the term. They are indebted people either by their own fault or by that of their fathers. They are at the service of their master towards whom they are indebted but they have the right to pay off the debt as soon as they can, or, if they are not happy with their master they also have the right to be bought by another master who then reimburses the previous one.

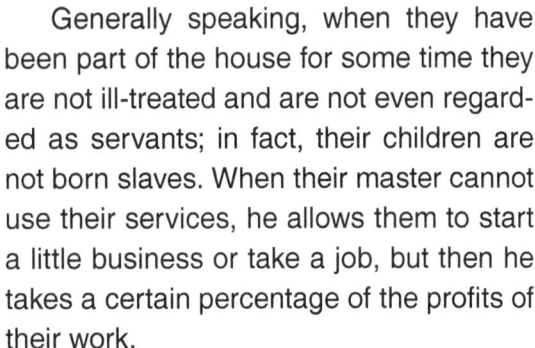

Generally speaking, when they have been part of the house for some time they are not ill-treated and are not even regarded as servants; in fact, their children are not born slaves. When their master cannot use their services, he allows them to start a little business or take a job, but then he takes a certain percentage of the profits of their work.

In addition to the indebted slaves there are the savages, called "Penongs" or "Stiengs" in Khmer whose trade is operated by the Laotians. Those people are

Uncivilized Man or "Penong"

slaves in the full sense of the word. They are called savages or forest men because they live in the wild between the left bank of the Mekong and the mountains of Cochin-China. In their environment they find more rice and maize than they need to feed themselves, almost without cultivating it or it is easy to cultivate. The rivers and the lakes provide them with fish in abundance; the forests they live in are populated with wild animals which they hunt, not with guns but with bows and arrows and all the other primitive ways of hunting. It takes them only a few hours to build their houses; a few bamboo sticks form the framework and the walls and the roofs are made of palm leaves attached to one another. As for their clothes, the above photograph gives an idea of what they are made of.

Men and women hide their nudity with a piece of cloth, the size of a vine leaf, held by two pieces of string tied around their waist. Sometimes however, during the big ceremonies, they wrap a piece of cloth around their waist which comes down to their knees. Their only desire of looking elegant resides in their use of earrings made of bones and large necklaces which adorn their chests. These are made of a piece of string and bits of bones.

They are quite happy in their wild ignorance. They have no intention of starting a revolution to change the form of a government; they are divided into villages having elderly men as chiefs.

They do not know how to write; some superstitions and rudimentary practices represent their religion; for them, God is the forest and its mysteries; they have no conception of how the stars move and as a consequence, have no means of measuring time.

They know two things only: "the earth which sees the rising of the sun and the country which the sun sets ablaze when it goes down;" that is to say, "sunrise and sunset."

The Laotians who are often at war with them capture them and sell them to the Cambodians. Those poor people are homesick most of the time; taken away from their forests and deprived of their freedom, they thus soon die. Those who managed to stand their homesickness and bear with their new condition become excellent servants for they are reliable and obliging.

Our French civilization started to decrease their numbers by rendering their trade more difficult and, before long, slavery was to become something of the past.

RELIGION - BUDDHISM

The prevailing religion in Cambodia is Buddhism as it is practiced in Ceylon [Sri Lanka] where it originated. It is taught by the Bonzes, also called 'Talapoints.' The latter wear a yellow [actually orange] outfit consisting of a large piece of cloth in which they wrap themselves, just as we would do with a big coat. They shave their heads and are busy exclusively with religion and live in monasteries next to pagodas where they teach children to read and write. They have very strict rules which they respectfully follow, meaning that they eat only once a day before midday and never after sunset; they drink nothing but water; they have to get up before day-break and cannot talk to women if there are fewer than three monks together. It can be a question of death should they disobey. They are forbidden to ask for anything, they are only allowed to receive what they are given without looking and uttering a word. Since they live only on charity, every morn-

Cambodian Bonzes

ing the monks go out carrying a kind of round tin box over their shoulder, covered with a piece of red cloth and a lid; they walk in a line, one behind another and visit each district of their parish in turn holding a lotus flower in their hand. In front of every house stands its master who, on a bench, has set up a big pot filled with steamed rice together with bananas, some fish and other types of food. The monk stops, turns his back not to see what is going to happen, hides his face with a fan and opens the box into which the person puts a spoonful of rice, some bananas and other pre-cooked dishes; then the monk closes it with the lid and walks to the next house, and so on and so forth until his box is full. Then he returns to the monastery.

In all circumstances of their lives, the people turn to them [the monks] to pray. In fact, they are obliged to answer all requests

The King's Pagoda

that are made of them. Their ministry consists in "theu bon" that is "doing good" and chasing away Arack (the devil). For this ceremony, they shout prayers at the top of their lungs. Very often these prayers are accompanied by horrible music and if the devil after all this commotion does not leave a house, it is because he really shows determination not to. What is rather strange is that they [the monks] can choose to be defrocked and either marry or go back to their wives for, although one is married, in Cambodia it is acceptable for a man to leave his wife for some time and go and repent in a monastery.

The King himself and all the other Mandarins have been bonzes once. Some bonzes, however, remain monks all their lives.

They are very respected by the Cambodian people who venerate them all the more because they follow the precepts of Buddhism without compunction.

The pagoda is a sort of monument built on strong wooden columns; its roof is on a steep incline and forms two superimposed floors; the photograph on page 15 represents the King's Pagoda located near his palace; the facade which can be seen above the entrance door is richly decorated with golden arabesques representing several heads of spirits. On either side of the entrance, a stone statue represents a guard armed with a club; the inside is composed of a single room only. On the walls there are paintings of the whole history of the Ramayana,

Guard of the Pagoda

a long poem in Sanskrit, the transcription of which is attributed to Valmiki. These pictures show the various episodes of the Ramayana; the combat between the good and the bad spirits; the combat of the monkeys who have the power to move mountains, the kidnapping of princesses; some views

Kidnapping of a Princess

of hell and paradise, etc., etc. At the far end of the temple one can see a big statue of Buddha made of stone and gold-colored wood, and on the side are other statues, smaller in size, made of bronze, silver or gold.

Statue of Buddha Made of Golden Bronze

The Cambodians visit the pagoda only on days of festival. So, in the New Year which takes place around the month of April, they go and wash the statues of Buddha and burn colorful candles which they place on small mounds of sand which act as candelabra. Among these festivals I would mention the agriculture festival, the religious ordination festival, during which the King presides over the joining of a religious order by his sons or his mandarins; the beginning of the rainy season in July; the big festival of offering to ancestors and lastly, a festival which consists in chasing evil spirits or chasing the devil, a festival which I talk about later on.

PHNOM-PENH - THE MEKONG

The capital of Cambodia is Phnôm-Penh (full mountain).

This town, the kingdom's big marketplace, is perfectly located, so much so that our government could not choose a better place to set up the Residence of the Protectorate's Representative.

As I mentioned earlier on, the crowning of the King took place in Oudong, a day's journey away north of Phnôm Penh. Oudong was the old capital; the Queen Mother still resided there when her son Norodom chose Phnôm Penh as the new capital for his kingdom in which the flag of the French Protectorate was already flying. Today Oudong is a dead town where all the monuments, palaces and pagodas, are going to ruin. Oudong's big pagoda, shown on the next page, was one of the prettiest pagodas in Cambodia.

Phnôm-Penh on the contrary kept growing and was embellished. It is the point where the king of the rivers, the Mekong, coming down from China splits into three arms: one which goes through lower Cochin-China and flows into the sea after crossing the province of Vinh-Long, the other running through Chaudoc to flow into the sea at Bassac, and the third river starting in Phnôm-Penh and going in the opposite direction to fill the big lake which we will discuss later on. The Mekong River, which has its source at the crossroads of Tibet and Koko-Nor, first flows from north to south under the name of Lang-san-Kiang and runs across the province of Yunnan (cloudy south) at its largest point. It is navigable from the longitude 22º and becomes one of the best communication routes for this province. However, the Chinese do not use it much to transport their products, they dread the wild populations who are under the domination of the Siam and fearing to see their boats being robbed or taxed outrageously by customs in Bangkok, they prefer to trade with the market of Bahmo on the Irrawaddy River. It is where the Lang-san-Kiang leaves the Yun-Mam Province that it becomes the Mekong River; after having

Pagoda at Oudong

flown through several tribal areas and Laos in particular, it turns into a magnificent river running in the middle of a fertile valley along which every year it lays down rich silt. Most of the soil is covered with forests, but there are also huge plains with herds of cows, buffaloes, elephants and rhinos.

At the level of longitude 18º, one can enjoy the ruins of Ventiane, the capital of the old kingdom of Laos which recognized the sovereignty of the Siam. The trade which was conducted in the past in this important city was later moved to the village of Nong-Kay. There, people used to buy horns, silk, ivory, wax, iron and silver. The money used was gold dust pushed inside tubes made of calao feathers and sealed with a cotton stamp. They weighed the gold dust with Chinese scales; in order to do so, they opened one end of the tube and poured the contents in the cavity of the upper part of the beak of a calao, its thin extremity allowing the powder to fall on the plate of the scale without losing one bit of it.

A Statue found in Sambor

Continuing down the river, one reaches Lakhon on the right bank; at that stage, the river is almost a kilometer wide. In Lakhon the marmorean clay rocks are exploited for the making of lime which is not very good for building, but which, on the other hand, is exported to the whole of Cambodia as the lime which the population chews together with the betel and the areca nut.

Continuing its flow towards the rapids of Khong, the Mekong River, narrowed between the mountains which separate them from the Annamese Empire and the possessions of Siam, it becomes more difficult to navigate. Going through uninhabited lands, it runs like a torrent trapped between high rocky embankments, rolling its waters over a base full of rocks that form such dangerous rapids that even the pirogues have problems making their way through these precipices. In order to get the goods through, people embark them up-river on strong rafts and they are loaded down-river on new small boats.

After passing through these cataracts, on its left bank, the Big River receives a considerable tributary: the Stung-Streng River, itself formed by several rivers coming down from the mountains of Cochin-China.

South of Khong, the Mekong River becomes navigable again when the water is high; the gun boats and the steam boats coming from Phnôm-Penh can sail up river all the way north of Stung-Streng.

A Cambodian Teapot
Made of Gold

From this village, the Mekong continues its fast flow along a beautiful and not so populated valley, in which not much trade is carried out, then, after passing Sambor, Samboc and two small Cambodian villages built on its left bank opposite Phnôm-Penh, at a point called the Four Arms, it flows on to the sea. The town of Phnôm-Penh therefore has been built at the confluence of the Four Arms of the Mekong including the mother arm. It is an exceptional situation rarely seen elsewhere. What is most striking in Cambodia in fact, is the beauty of this Big River with its periodic swelling which happens around the month of September. Then, the waters rise up to 10 or 12 meters and inundate the plains where they lay their silt.

The population of Phnôm-Penh, about thirty-five thousand inhabitants, is composed of Cambodians, Chinese, Annamese, Malay, Malabar and a few Europeans. Most houses were built by the King who, in the past, rented them to French people because he alone could be landlord in his kingdom; but recently, thanks to the intervention of our Governor General, Mr. de Lanessan, the right to own private property was created, new streets were opened and important transactions were made on the pieces of land. This reform, which was the most important that could have been made in Cambodia, was to contribute to the wealth of this beautiful country and our settlers never forgot that they were indebted to Mr. de Lanessan for being the first to have the initiative and the know-how to make the King understand that by rendering the land of his kingdom alienable, it meant opening a new way to our commerce and to our industry. It is difficult to get attached to a country where one does business without having solid links there.

The right to own property has already attracted many merchants to Cambodia who started to use their capital to buy plots of land on which they built their commercial houses.

About twenty years ago, when I arrived in Phnôm-Penh, there were only few brick houses in the town; people lived in huts made of bamboo and straw; they hardly needed two days to erect these buildings. The representative of the Protectorate himself lived on the riverside in a hut which was far from being as comfortable as the actual Residence. Today, between the King's palace and the buildings of the Protectorate which are located at both ends of the town, European style houses have risen everywhere and before long Phnôm-Penh will look like a small image of Saigon, the capital of Cochin-China. Among the recent developments we find: the new 'Kampot Street' entirely built up, Piquet Street, Verneville Street, a few side roads and a big indoor market made of iron. I must also mention a canal which was dug in the center of town and which, taking its water from the river, then flows back into the same river downstream from Phnôm-Penh after bypassing the town. Three bridges allow its crossing to reach the various districts. Up until now this canal, due to its shallowness, did not serve to the extent people expected it would. It should be dug even deeper but one fears that once the money has been spent, one is confronted by new difficulties, for the current coming from the river certainly will erode its 10 to 12-meter embankments and concrete banks will have to be built, which means considerable expense.

The poor people live on boats on the riverbank. These people generally make a living from small commerce, buying rice, fish and other products which they go and get inland and then sell. They can easily travel as they please, their boats being their means of transport and lodging at the same time.

In the market in Phnôm-Penh one finds tobacco, pepper seeds from Kampot, sugar cane, ginger, indigo, areca nuts, betel, resin, lacker, rice, silk, mattresses and mats. These latter two articles are a speciality of the country and are highly sought-after. The 5 to 15-centimeter-thick mattresses are made of cellulose fibre. This is the produce of a tree which grows very easily and gives pods containing a very silky cotton. To make these mattresses, the fibre is inserted in a sheet divided in compartments. This is a process which allows one to fold the mattress and reduce its volume to the smallest size possible. When people want to use it, all they have to do is unfold it. The mats are made of strong artificially coloured rush and mixed with other types of naturally coloured yellow rush. In this way, very pretty patterns appear.

These mats, which are 1.60m long by 70 to 80 cm wide, are spread on bamboo beds used by the indigenous people or on the floor for them to sit on; they have a long life.

I must also mention Cambodian jewelry manufacturing which has a very particular original character. The King has jewel makers who know how to admirably work gold and silver, and who are excellent at setting precious stones to make rings, necklaces and other accessories.

Goods which in the past were bartered, are now purchased with money in the form of silver bars, Cambodian and Mexican piastres, and new coins which the King had stamped for a few years. Moreover, bank notes from the Bank of Indochina are used as well as piastres especially stamped for Cochin-China and are in circulation all over Cambodia.

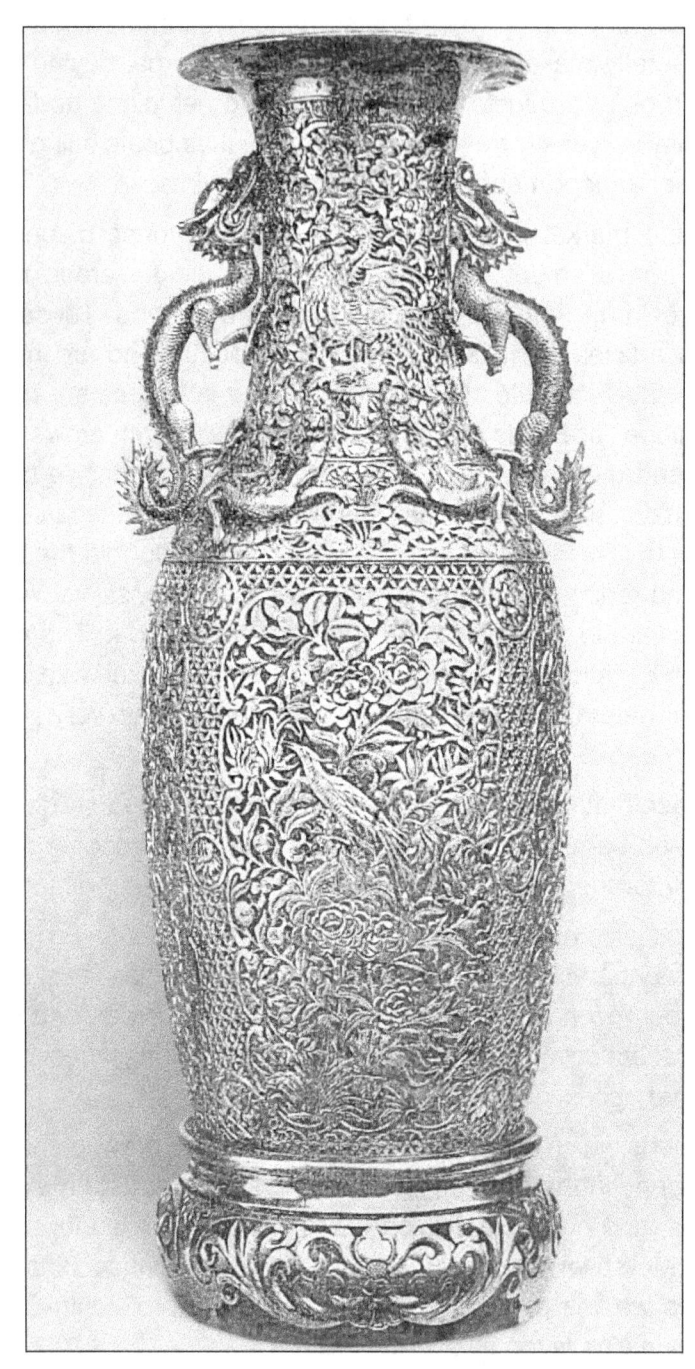

A Vase Made of Silver

The bar called 'nêne' is a silver ingot measuring 15 cm in length by 3 cm in width and 1 cm in thickness, it is worth about 50 francs. As for the Cambodian piastres called 'Bât', they appear in various types, one being less wide but thicker than the other. Their value however is the same, four francs. I insisted on giving a facsimile because, today, they are very rare and have been replaced by the new currency which comprises silver coins with values of two francs, one franc, fifty cents respectively and copper coins with values of ten and five cents.

As we can see, the stamping of these coins is based on our monetary system.

Four Coins

A Cambodian Plate Made of Tooled Copper

CAMBODIA'S HABITS AND CUSTOMS

Travellers who go from Saigon, in Viet Nam, to Cambodia are amazed at the difference in race existing between these two neighboring countries.

The Annamese are small, Cambodian people are tall. The Annamese are dressed from head to foot, minus the shoes however; the Cambodian only wear a piece of cloth wrapped around their waist. They do not have the same religion; one could say that the Annamese are Buddhist, but for those who know them and who have lived among them a while, it is easy to recognize that they have only one particular and religiously observed cult, it is the "cult of the ancestors." They mock their priests with revolting casualness, whereas the Cambodian have a great respect for theirs.

Religions being different, so are habits; as for the languages they have no similarity. It would be like comparing a Breton and a Southerner speaking French in France. The Annamese language is musical, the Cambodian language is *recto tono*, as easy to understand as the Malay language.

The Annamese wear their hair long. The Cambodian shave their heads leaving a flat-top tuft of hair only to ornate their cranium. Their religion, their language, their habits and the type of the Cambodian race would appear to come, just like the Siamese race, from a mixture of Indian and Malay; only the Indian blood would dominate among the Cambodians whereas in the Siamese it would be the Malay. If, after comparing the Cambodians with the Annamese, we continue the same comparison with their other neighbors, for example, the Siamese, we see that the difference is not the same anymore. Except perhaps for the language, particularly the general language, for the titles and the words used in the royal court and in the prayers are the same; the kingdom of Cambodia and the kingdom of Siam present a strong analogy. All the ceremonies and festivities are conducted in the same way in both countries. One would recognize Siamese by their weak and lazy appearance; the Cambodian would seem less servile. They are tall, muscular; they have a pug nose, high cheek-bones and a soft look in their eyes. As for their hair it deserves a particular mention. Cambodian men and women alike shave off their hair, keeping a tuft only on top of their head and maintained short, from 4 to 5 centimeters. Only women let grow a lock of hair called 'Prouit.' It is on either side of their temples, coming down onto their shoulders.

Women's speech is softer than that of the men's, the tone of their voice is somewhat imploring.

The complexion of the Cambodian is dark. It is due to the fact that they never wear a hat and despite their shaven head they stand in the sun in any temperature. Men and women wear the same fundamental outfit, the 'Sâmpot'; it is a small piece of material which they wrap around their waist and then pull its long pleats passing between the legs to tie them up at the waist at the back. Women, on top of the 'Sâmpot,' wear a scarf, like a chain, around their neck in order to hide their breasts.

A Cambodian Woman

Such is the outfit of the ordinary people. The Mandarins, for their part, add a short jacket either made of cotton or silk, depending on their degree of wealth; that tight jacket is tied at the front by seven buttons and it becomes compulsory to wear as soon as they enter the palace.

I was the first to import into Cambodia the cotton fabric from Rouen and Roanne to make 'Sâmpots.' Today it is a common article bought by all Cambodian people; however, I must add that on days of celebration 'rich' people and the Mandarins dress in the "Sâmpot haul" which is made of woven silk and adorned with original designs. Every woman knows how to weave, and since in every home there is a loom, they are the ones who are in charge of making clothes for their husbands for the days of festivities.

In Cambodia everybody chews betel, even very young children as soon as they start walking. One needs three things to chew betel: its leaf, some pink colored slaked lime, and the nut of areca. The betel is some kind of creeping pepper bush, the green leaves of which resemble our lilac leaves. People pick them before they turn yellow, then they are collected in packets of twenty or thirty and sold in the streets or in the "wet" market. The nut of areca is the fruit from a kind of palm tree with slender stems which possesses very astringent properties. As for the lime, and as I mentioned earlier, it comes from the limestone of Lakhon in the big rivers.

The custom of chewing betel is so important to the Cambodians that they constantly carry the necessary ingredients with them; poor people carry them in a copper case, the rich ones carry silver or even gold cases. These boxes measuring 12 to 15 cm are divided in compartments in which the nut, the leaves and the slaked lime are placed, plus a small spatula. In order to prepare a "chew," one takes a betel leaf, spreads a little bit of lime on it with the spatula, adds some slices of the nut of areca then the whole lot is rolled as a cigarette and it is put in one's mouth.

All that remains to do is to chew, an activity which can last a good half hour. This mastication in no time at all produces a bright red saliva which stains the lips. One is inclined to believe that the betel does not irritate the digestive tracts as one could imagine, otherwise people would not consume it so much. The sole inconvenience which seems to result from chewing betel is the loosening of teeth and, if I may say so, the plating of the palate resulting in a sense of taste considerably dulled, to such an extent that the Cambodian cannot, without making a grimacing face, drink some absinthe, some bitter and all sorts of pure alcohol in the same way as we do when we drink water.

According to the observations of numerous doctors, betel prevents fevers and dysentery, and should increase the tone of one's skin and through its astringent action should prevent excessive sweating which tends to weaken the inhabitants of hot countries. Since chewing involves spitting a lot, when people indulge in this pleasure, even inside their huts, people make sure they always have a small copper urn next to them which they use as a spittoon; as a consequence, when there are several people together, from these spittoons, acrid smell comes up which makes one gag and which the Europeans find difficult to get used to.

People also smoke a lot in Cambodia. Tobacco, one of the local products, is bad for one. It does not burn well and has no aroma. Despite this and since one can smoke while chewing betel, men, women and children alike do that all-day long. Cigarettes are in the shape of the leaves in which the tobacco is consumed. It is rolled up inside pieces of light-brown banana leaves, making sure that one of the extremities is bigger than the other just as with the cigarettes of Manila. Women are generally in charge of rolling cigarettes for household consumption. They fasten them in their middle with a thin thread so that they do not come loose.

One can buy ready-made cigarettes from hawkers who stand in the streets or in market places. In order not to have to continually pull cigarettes out of their case placed in one of the pleats of the 'Sâmpot' belt, the smokers take three at a time, one of them going straight into their mouth and the other two at the back of each ear waiting to be smoked.

The food of the Cambodian is made up of steamed rice, a staple replacing our bread, and salt fish, fruit, vegetables, poultry and meat from the animals they can hunt. These are: deer, stag, wild boar and wild elephant. The hunters are very brave. I have seen some who succeeded in killing elephants with bad slingshots which cost 10 francs. When the elephants during the night make their way down from the mountains to go and eat in the sugar cane plantations, the hunters go and surprise them at dawn, quietly crawling closer to them against the wind and once they've arrived close to an elephant they fire a bullet into its ear. If the shot is successful, the animal drops dead; on the contrary, if the hunter does not have time to run away, the hunter's days are very limited, for with one hit with its trunk the elephant can knock him over and trample him.

Although the flesh of the elephant is not tender, people dry it in the sun and salt it as they do the meat of other animals.

A Palenquin to Mount on an Elephant's Back

The trunk and the feet are royal dishes generally served to the sovereign. I tasted some several times at the King's table, but I must admit that this highly sought-after dish, to me, is not very appetizing.

Some people still hunt elephants in another way, but when they do so, it is to reduce them to captivity and turn them into domestic animals. To capture them they go to areas which the elephants frequent, taking with them large domesticated elephants which will attract their compatriots. Once they are gathered together, they surround the young elephants, then men pass chains between the elephants' legs and take them away to train them to carry loads. In actual fact, they are very helpful in a country where the only means of communication are rivers.

With an elephant one can go everywhere; it finds it way through forests, bushes and swamps. No obstacle can stop it.

With its trunk it pushes aside every thing that is in its way, it goes over rocks, swims across the widest rivers carrying travellers on its back in a kind of cage. When riding one is certainly strongly shaken, sometimes going forward, sometimes being shaken from right to left, sometimes from left to right, and people who are not used to this are usually sick. Because an elephant can cost between five hundred and two thousand francs, it is well taken care of; it is fed with new grass, banana leaves and sugar cane which it enjoys very much.

I cannot pass over the white elephant in silence. White elephants are relatively rare and are always offered to the King when people find some in the forest. They are not really white as one could imagine. They are simply different from the other elephants because of their eyes which, instead of being black, are brighter, just like the eyes of albinos, and because of the white marks which seem to have come out on their body as a result of some skin disease. A few years ago, the King was in possession of two white elephants; they were in a special stable where servants fed them with sugar cane and cakes served on silver dishes. Besides that, from the very moment they are captured, white elephants are highly revered. They are taken to the King accompanied by music and with ceremony; on the top sit these servants. They have musicians especially assigned to serve them and take them for a bath every day; a mandarin opens a large yellow parasol over their heads, and the musicians preceding them open the route for them. If they fall ill, they are treated by a doctor of the court, and bonzes say prayers for them.

There exists another mode of transport to travel inland in Cambodia, it is the [ox] cart; very primitively built, the travellers are horribly shaken in it. One should say that since there is no fear for the nonexistent suspension, it rides everywhere, in the potholes of the roads, in the ravines, through the bushes and even in the shallow streams.

An Ox Cart

But let us return to the Cambodian people. Their houses, as the picture at the beginning of this chapter shows, are built on stilts, first as a matter of sanitation and second to protect the inhabitants from flooding which, every year, inundates the land above the embankments. The whole framework is made of bamboo, only the houses of the mandarins include parts made of hard wood; the roof has a steep slope allowing the water to run down during the rainy season and the walls are made of palm leaves assembled in the shape of screens joined together by bamboo lintels. The entrance door leads to the main room, the reception room; foreigners never enter the other rooms which are reserved only for family members. The houses being so light and constructed with material which can be set on fire by a slight spark, they are thus often engulfed in flames and when the wind starts blowing, in no time at all a whole district can be destroyed; it is true that rebuilding requires little time.

In terms of medicine, Cambodian people are rather backward. Their doctors, called "Krou-Pêts", most of the time resort to the Chinese pharmacopeia; they don't know much about the diseases which they treat with plasters made of ground herbs; they rub the wounds with a mixture of oil, gunpowder and green leaves. Delivering babies is done by Cambodian midwives who enjoy a good reputation. A strange custom consists in placing the mother on a floor formed by a bamboo mat with gaps underneath under which is a fire, in a stove, which is lit to burn perfume. This improvised bed is delimited by a cotton thread forming a barrier which one is allowed to pass only after a certain time. This thread has the power to chase away the evil spirits; yet, delivering babies is carried out successfully.

I will put an end to this quick study of Cambodian habits with the description of their funerals which is all the more interesting because cremating someone, very common all over Cambodia, has been adopted (now) in Paris where sophisticated furnaces have been established for a few years. Now the custom of cremation, which the Greeks and the Romans practiced, was abolished by the Christians. The respect that we had for the dead made us believe that the flames of the ancient stake were repulsive; but modern science with its safe and fast devices managed in just a few instants to do the hideous work of decomposition which used to take place in the ground, far from our eyes. The furnaces in Paris indeed bear no resemblance to the cremations that are still carried out in Siam or in Cambodia. When a Cambodian person is close to dying, his or her family goes and fetches the bonzes who come to say prayers. If these do not prevent the death of the person, once the sad spectacle of witnessing the death has taken place, the cadaver is washed in order to purify it, then it is wrapped from head to toe in a piece of raw cotton. Some kind of silver or gold object is put inside its mouth and the body is put inside a coffin which will be placed on the grill. Poor people burn their dead immediately, middle class people keep them for three or four days. As for the rich, they keep them longer depending on their wealth and according to certain precepts of hygiene.

So, they start cremation by taking out the guts which are thrown over to the dogs; then, after having injected some mercury in the cavity of the stomach, they put the body in the coffin and, through a hole dug into the lid, they introduce a long hollow piece of bamboo which by going up to the top of the house, is used as a ventilation pipe or as a draught.

On the chosen day for the cremation, which generally takes place in a yard close to the house, the coffin escorted by the bonzes saying prayers, and by the members of the family and by friends is put on a huge iron grill above the unlit pyre. The bonze presiding over the ceremony asks for the top of the coffin to be removed, he then lights the fire where the head is resting and the bearers set the four corners under the coffin on fire; then the family members throw fragrant wood such as sandal wood onto the fire. While the body is burning, cries and sobs can be heard. The next day, when the fire is out, children come with urns made either of clay or copper in which they put the ashes and the remaining bones.

For the members of the royal family, this type of ceremony is important. The King waits until he has a certain number of dead persons to burn together. The bodies are kept for one year and often several years. In this meantime, the biggest trees that can be found in the forests are chopped down and the mandarins start making a colossal catafalque with a pyramidal shaped top which is then placed within the wall surrounding the palace; at the given time for the ceremony public entertainment starts and lasts several days. The cremation takes place afterwards. The coffins are then open to see in which state the bodies are; often they are not completely dry. In this case the skin is pealed off, the King then lights the pyre, and the ashes and the bones are placed into gold vases which are put in the royal pagoda, near the palace.

CELEBRATIONS

After having dealt with such a sad topic as the one I have just written about, let us leave the dead to rest in peace and get back to the living. I will now talk about their (Cambodian) festivals. Although numerous, they are often sumptuous and can last for three days. To us, the most peculiar one is the festival consisting of driving the Arak (the devil) away from the palace. To do so, all the assistants wrap cotton headbands given by the King around their heads. Similar bands (such as the head-bands) surround the royal apartments and are stretched like telegraphic wires all around the outside of the palace. Only on such circumstances do the bonzes refrain from praying; instead and at given intervals, they let out screams which are signals for the soldiers of the King indicating that they can start fires and firing canon balls against bad spirits. In that way the devil is invited to leave following which the cotton bands, once the festival is over, are cut up in pieces and worn as bracelets by the assistants.

One of the most beautiful festivals is the water festival, which takes place after the periodical rising of the Big River, when the waters having reached the highest level form a vast currentless lake. The boat races feature the Mandarins who each provide a boat which is brought by his servants. These boats, measuring sometimes 30 meters in length, accommodate 40 paddlers who, sitting in twos on the same bench, move their frail skiff by dipping a paddle into the water extremely rapidly using both hands.

In order to paddle in time, they accompany their movements with chants written for the occasion. The paddler at the back constantly maintains his paddle in the water and, by moving it to the left or to the right, fulfils the role of a rudder. Generally, he is the most skillful, for a false move could cause the boat to overturn. These boats can reach a tremendous speed. One year a Mandarin bet that he would reach Saigon before the steamboat of the shipping line which regularly sails between Phnôm-Penh

A Canoe for the Races

and Saigon; the journey took two days, and the paddlers' boat arrived in Saigon six hours before the steamboat.

The King watches the races with his whole suite from a junk; after each race, the paddlers come to pay their respect to him. In the evening around one hundred boats decorated with multicolored Chinese lanterns, with singers and musicians on board, sail past the stand of officials surrounded by fireworks illuminating the whole river.

I must now talk about the dance exhibitions that the King organizes inside his palace in a special room called 'the dance theater'. At the slightest opportunity, the King orders a performance which lasts all night. More than a hundred female dancers appear on stage, they perform pantomimes and singers perform songs which tell about the past splendors of the famous kingdom of the Khmers at the time it also comprised Siam and Laos.

The costumes, the price of which often reaches 10,000 francs, are splendid; embroideries, gold and precious stones shine in front of the spectators' eyes with every move that the dancers make.

Characters Performing in Cambodian Dances

A very special music accompanies the songs and the contortions of the performers. The drawing above, made by a Cambodian artist, gives an accurate idea of what the dancers were like; their nails are adorned with silver claws, sometimes they wear sandals which imitate the feet of fantastic animals and the golden wings placed on their hips make them look like angels.

The musicians strike various kinds of xylophones, the keyboards of which are made of wood; they also play a big wooden flute equipped with a reed like the one on our clarinets.

This instrument accompanied by drums gives high-pitched and low-pitched sounds, and the musician playing the important instrument sits in the middle of a circle. The instrument made of

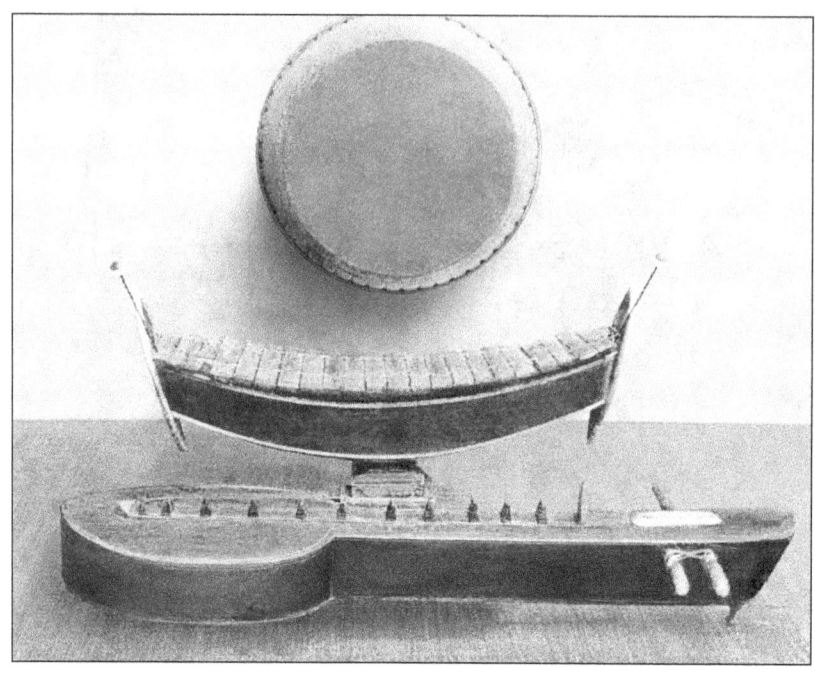

Guitar - Xylaphone - Tam Tam

bamboo bears twenty-one copper cymbals suspended on ropes with, in its middle, a mushroom-like bulge which the musician strikes with both hands and with the help of light wooden or cork hammers. The King takes great pleasure in seeing these dances being performed. The French after having marvelled at the strange outfits of the actresses, end up finding the scenes which they do not understand, quite monotonous.

A Cambodian Musician and Instruments

Characters Performing in Cambodian Dances

FISHING ON THE GREAT LAKE

Earlier we described the Mekong River, which at the level of Phnôm-Penh, flows into the sea via two arms; moreover, it forms a third one which, due to a unique phenomenon, seems to go back up river parallel to the main arm.

This phenomenon happens from August to November, when the waters rise, coming down extremely fast from the main arm. Not finding enough space to escape through the two inferior arms leading to the sea, it then flows backwards and forms a huge lake, the Tonle-Sap lake, where fish come and take refuge.

To go from Phnôm-Penh to the lake, fishermen take advantage of the beginning of the reverse of the flow of water: all they

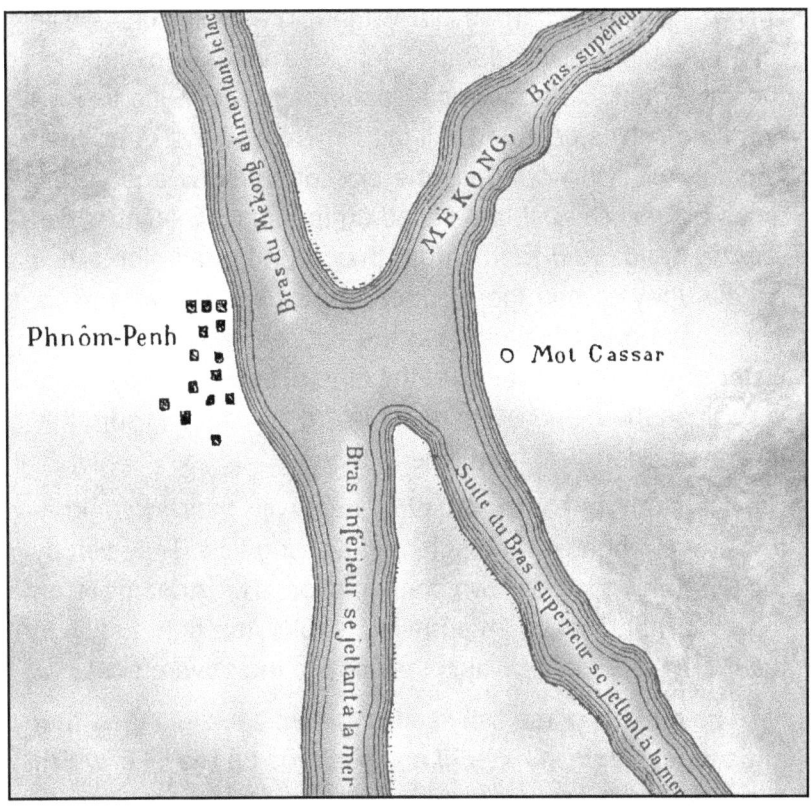

The Four Branches of the Mekong

have to do then is steer their boats which, carried along by the current, arrive without effort upstream at the fishing site. When they have finished fishing, because the volume of the water diminishes, the lake empties itself. The current then runs from north to south, so the fishermen use it to sail back to Phnôm-Penh the way from which they came originally. The current pushes the boats along. This arm of the Mekong therefore presents an amazing spectacle, that of going from south to north, during a few months to fill up the lake; then, once the lake is full, the current goes back to its starting point to flow into the sea.

This lake is the richness of the country for the fish it contains are sufficient in quantity to supply the whole of Cochin-China. Fishing is carried out without great difficulty. Each boat is equipped with bamboo fences and large nets which the fishermen use to delimit a vast area in which the fish will find themselves captured. All the fishermen have to do then is catch the fish which are the size of salmons and sometimes bigger. The fish are salted on the spot. The fishermen cut the heads and the fins off, they then cut all along their middle, they spread them out on racks held up by bamboo. The bamboo is slightly above the surface of the water (the water is about 1.50m deep at the time of fishing). They sprinkle salt on them and let them dry in the sun making sure that they are turned over from time to time.

It is strange that the Cambodians, with their sweet apathy, do not engage in commerce involving fish. They fish by the river only for their own consumption. The Annamese on the other hand, more enterprising, exploit the right to fish in the Big Lake for a fee which they pay to the government.

The residue of the fish itself is thrown back into the water and attracts a big number of aquatic birds on the lake, which is surrounded by magnificent forests.

Crocodiles are in abundance too; the Annamese chase them all the way to the Big River to send them back to Cochin-China where they are in great demand as food in the indigenous market places. This chase, rather productive for those who do it, is very strange; a man and two children are enough to control these reptiles which can be three meters long. On board a little pirogue, they sail along the river dragging behind them at the bottom of the water a net made of steel and attached to a piece of rattan. As soon as the crocodile gives some resistance to the Annamese fishermen, they direct the boat towards the riverbank and on a sandbar where the crocodile lets itself be pulled without too much reluctance. After that, when its head starts sticking out of the water, one of the children, with an incredible boldness, jumps on it and in the twinkling of an eye muzzles its jaws with a rattan rope. The trickiest part is then over, for the animal not being able to grab its prey defends itself only with its tail. However, the Annamese man, while being careful, bends the front legs of the animal and ties them up on its back; all that remains is to entirely pull the crocodile out of the water onto the sand and to tie the back legs to the tail.

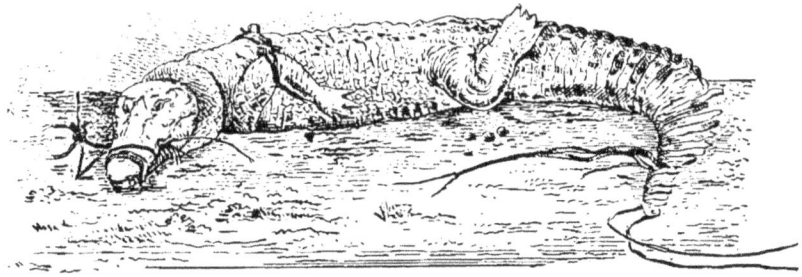

A Trussed Crocodile

The crocodile, as shown in the above picture, is provisionally placed on the bottom of a boat filled with water and, when there is a whole load, they are taken to the market places in Cochin-China to the delight of the Annamese consumers.

THE RUINS OF ANGKOR

At one end of the big lake (mentioned above) are huge forests filled with game. After going through them towards the northeast, over a few kilometers, through the vines, one can spot the remains of an ancient roadway made of cut stones. This roadway which, in the past, must have been gigantic, was probably the road leading to Angkor-Thôm, the old capital of the famous kingdom of the Khmer whose ruins act as a witness to a glorious past. According to tradition, the King's palaces alone covered an area measuring several leagues. This very king had 3 million soldiers and governed about one hundred other dependent kings!

How is it that such a large population disappeared leaving only a small kingdom behind them?

Mouhot, who died in 1858 after having explored part of the Mekong River, was the first French person to visit the Ruins of Angkor-Thôm. Here is what he said in recounting his journey:

> At the sight of these temples one's mind feels overwhelmed, one's imagination overcome; one looks, admires, and, full of respect, one remains silent; for where can one find words to praise an architectural work which has never had its equivalent anywhere on the globe?

The first striking object is a huge door opening onto two interior galleries. From then on, the eyes only perceive palaces, pagodas, foundations which are 60 meters thick, with upper galleries, also a wealth of incredible ornamentation. One single monument comprises thirty-four towers; one would need several months to have an accurate idea of all these wonders.

As for the Cambodians, some say that the angels are the creators of this construction. Others, and I believe they are right, attribute the origin to the famous leprous King (Neac Somdack Comlong), who probably had them built to pay a bonze for his promise of his (the King's) recovery from leprosy. It would be the latter who also had the pagoda of the town of Angkor built. His

The Ruins of Angkor

statue stands there, and strikes everyone by the nobility of its physiognomy. Experts think that these monuments were probably erected during the ninth century, when the kingdom of Cambodia was at the peak of its glory.

Three hours walking through a forest are needed to reach a platform composed of huge stones perfectly placed edge to edge; beautiful stairs can be found at intervals with ornaments representing a sphinx. Four main staircases give access to this magnificent promenade, from which runs along a 250 meters long by 10 meters wide roadway with supporting walls made of granite. One then reaches a moat with a huge perimeter which surrounds all those buildings. One walks over a bridge and arrives at an area where trees have not been able to grow and where there is a magnificent five-tower colonnade. The middle tower is the highest and is outlined against the sky. It is of a prodigious height.

All this is elegant and stately, and when one looks at these ruins very carefully, one finds perfection and gracious beauty for there is not one stone, one single tile which has not been carved, as we can see by looking with a magnifying glass at the photoengraving shown on the previous page. In this huge maze of monuments, one comes across enormous blocks forming cupolas, domes which were probably gilded since one can still spot remains of colors. One is seized with respect for the workers who managed to find strong enough methods to lift these gigantic monuments to such considerable heights. In fact, a general map could be imagined by drawing two huge squares, one inside the other and surrounded by galleries from which four roads start and end up at the monument in the center. In the middle there is a statue which is still worshipped by the bonzes and around which the Cambodians and the Siamese hold some ceremonies. There are twenty-four obelisks surrounding these main monuments. Last but not least, we must pause to look at columns, lions, elephants and fantastic animals made of granite and the triumphal arches.

The surrounding wall of this town which is in ruins has a pe-

The Ruins of Angkor

The Ruins of Angkor

rimeter of 40 km, is 8 meters high (in places it is even 15 meters high) and 3 meters thick. It has five gates, two of them facing east. Almost all the bas-reliefs are made up of four superposed plans representing a king watching wars and dances where ladies are always in large number.

A Lodge for Travellers

In India there exist statues of an absolutely identical type, and this is not surprising for Buddhism, originating in India, is also the religion of Cambodia. A bridge comprising fourteen arches which seems most ancient is also striking because of the ingenious way it was built. All these monuments are covered with a large quantity of characters written in Pali which are still quite visible; until now they have not been deciphered. People pretend that they are the key, which one absolutely has to decipher. As always, there exist legends which people tell; so, for example, people show a stone which they say communicates with the sea and moves when the sea is rough.

Be that as it may, this grandiose architecture would baffle any scientist, any archeologist who could search the past to make it talk. It is most regrettable that such monuments went into ruin, for, even in the state they are in, any person lucky enough to be able to contemplate them has to bow in their presence.

Bas-Relief from the ruins of Angkor

PRODUCTS OF CAMBODIA

TOBACCO

Tobacco grows almost everywhere in Cambodia. There the plant reaches a large size. Its stem is almost twice as big as the same plant which is cultivated in Sumatra. It is not unusual to see leaves measuring 60 or 65 centimeters in length by 40 centimeters in width. Unfortunately, no matter what care has been taken till now for its preparation, the tobacco exported from Cambodia to the markets of Europe has been judged too rich in nicotine and not easily smoked. These two imperfections may not be irreparable, but they have nevertheless and for a certain time hampered the chances which this industry could have had to develop in the country.

PEPPER

Pepper production is very successful in several provinces. We will mention the provinces of Kampot, Peam and Treang. These last few years, due to exaggerated taxes on the importing of pepper into France no matter their origin, a situation was created where our plantations were fighting the foreign competition and the culture of this spice was hampered. A reduction of duty of 1.04 francs per kilogram granted since 1891 to the importation of pepper from our colonies into France not only protected Cambodian plantations from ruin, something they dreaded, but also gave hope of great profits to those who exploited pepper. Today, the number of indigenous planters has increased rapidly. It is one crop which might be worthwhile for the French to attract immigrants to Cambodia who have some capital.

COFFEE

Coffee grows easily in several provinces, notably those on the Gulf of Siam and the Big River (the Mekong). It is of the type known as "Liberia" which seems to be the most resistant and the most appropriate to the country. But the plantations are very recent and have not yet reached a period of full yield. Nevertheless, one is already allowed to have great hopes for that culture. The young plants grow beautifully and after only fifteen months flowers and fruit have appeared on the shrubs. Therefore, there is no reason here to fear the failures which struck the first enterprises which were attempted in Cochin-China and the memory of which has far too long paralysed the initiative of the settlers.

THE MULBERRY TREE

On the edges of the Big River, Cambodian people engage in the cultivation of a dwarf mulberry tree whose branches are cut off level with the ground every year. Silk, fabricated with primitive processes, is not abundant enough and presents too many imperfections to be sold on European markets. Its color and solidity are unparalleled. Perhaps by improving the race of the silkworms and by perfecting the process of "suffocation" of the cocoons, the French capitalists could find their use in the exportation of these cocoons to Europe.

COTTON

Cotton, known in China since the earliest centuries, has always been carefully cultivated in Cambodia, on the edges of the Big River and on the island of Kassuthine, north of Phnom-Penh. Its culture is made easy because every year, when the Mekong rises, the soil is fertilized by the silt which the water lays. As a consequence, the harvest is abundant. However, the quality of the Cambodian cotton is not the best. This is probably due to the lack of care from the people. A really serious enterprise has very recently been created on the island of Kassuthine. A Frenchman, Mr. Praire, has installed a very large enterprise for the threshing of cotton, and has succeeded beautifully. The tax on the export of this merchandise is levied according to its weight. Mr. Praire had the ingenious idea of separating the seed from the cotton in order to reduce the tax and he is certain, in doing so, to have an excellent result given the fact that 25% of the weight of Cambodian cotton is in its seeds.

After the threshing, the seeds are utilized to make an oil which is good to consume while fresh and which is mainly used in France for the preparation of sardines in oil. The success obtained by Mr. Praire will certainly encourage other settlers to venture into this kind of industry which is bound to have a good future.

CARDAMOM

Cardamom is a tall and beautiful perennial plant with trailing roots which gives small ovoid capsules and grows in Cambodia in humid places. It is similar to ginger. Its seed is frequently used as medicine by the indigenous people as it is said to have digestive properties, and Chinese people regard it as a very powerful aphrodisiac.

Cardamom can be found on the borders with Siam on the mountain sides exposed to the rising sun, in the middle of thick, cold, damp and unhealthy forests.

Cambodian people are very fond of the tuberous roots that grow in abundance at the base of the cardamom plant; they boil them for several hours and with the water impregnated with the aroma of the roots, they make a drink which is popular all over the country. This drink has the property of giving vigor and warmth to the body.

There are two kinds of cardamom, the cultivated kind and the wild one. The sale of the first kind is much more expensive. Before selling the seeds, they are heated on a bamboo trellis underneath on which a fire is lit to help separate them from the pod. They then are the size of a chickpea. It is in the province of Pursat that business is transacted with this product.

IRON ORE

The most important deposit in Cambodia, the only one which until now has been the object of a serious study, is in the province of Phnom-Penh at Kompong-Soai. It is exploited by the Kouy, an uncivilized population of the region, in a very primitive way using very costly processes. Their very much appreciated products assume the shape of small bars stretched at both ends and is used as currency all over Laos as well as in a large part of Siam. According to studies done in 1881 and 1882 by Mr. Fuchs, civil mining engineer, "... the selected ores are perfectly suitable for the new methods of the metallurgy of the iron and can produce excellent Bessmer or Martin steels, in the best possible conditions". The ore is an oxide of iron containing about 70% metal, according to tests carried out in the laboratory of the 'Forges et Ateliers de Commentry'.

The evaluation of the importance of the deposit, carried out by the same engineer, shows up to 6 or 7 million tons of ore.

TORTOISE SHELL

The Caret tortoise provides a shell which can be sold commercially; it is an article very much used in the Parisian industry.

Fishing the Caret tortoise is practiced on the coasts of the islands of the Gulf of Siam located west and south-west of Phuquoc.

It takes place around the month of December, when the

A Caret Turtle

north-east monsoon is well in place and finishes in April with the south-west monsoon.

The boats which are used for this kind of fishing belong to the ports of Hatien (Cochin-China) and Kampot (Cambodia).

The products are sold in these two towns although it is impossible to exactly determine the annual value of that fishing which is almost entirely monopolized by some Chinese merchants from Kampot.

This particular article is sold in China at very advantageous prices. The scales of the shells of the Caret tortoise are independent from one another and set just like roof tiles. They can vary from blond to blackish in color. The blond variety is the more sought after and the more expensive of the two.

The prepared tortoises are sold on the spot for ten piastres each, depending on their size.

DEPOSITS OF SALTPETER, LIME AND CLAY

In the provinces of Pheam and Kampot, on the island of Khamaou and in Phnom-Sa, one finds deposits of limestone and saltpeter which have only been exploited by indigenous people. On the Big River, north of Krauchmar there exist quarries of kaolin, which until now have never been profitable. The lime of limestone coming from Cambodia is very appreciated in Cochin-China and preferred to the lime of sea-shells from Singapore.

OUR CURRENT SITUATION IN CAMBODIA IN 1894

During more or less the first twenty years which followed the treaty signed between Vice Admiral de la Grandiere and King Norodom (a treaty which placed the latter under the protectorate of France), our political and economic role in Cambodia was almost nil because all it involved for the French was simply having a representative in Phnom-Penh who depended for direction on the Governor of Cochin-China.

The King administered his states as he pleased, trying by any means to escape as much as possible the supervision of France. Our representatives, for their part, either through indolence or inability, were quite happy to quickly put an end to their stay serving the Cambodian King in order to be granted an extra promotion and return to France. As for the development of our trade, it was the least of their worries. Mr. Moura who rose from being a quartermaster, had reached the grade of "Lieutenant of vessel," had the honor of representing us in Cambodia during about twelve years. One can say without hesitation that these were years lost for France. Narrow-minded but ambitious, Mr. Moura used all his intelligence to prevent interaction between the King and the (French) Governor without bothering about reforms which obviously were necessary. It was with a certain terror that he saw (French) traders arriving in Phnom-Penh and trying to place themselves in some major cities. These "merchants of wigs," these "brothers from the coast," as he called them, to him were like the "Sword of Damocles" hanging over his head.

Without having any influence on the King, without even having managed to learn the local language after a long stay in the country, he (the French Governor) understood one thing only: colonies were made to allow officers to be promoted and not to help our export trade. The result of such apathy was that since the King was not receiving any advice, since he was not given any guidelines, he (the King) handed over his reins to his Mandarins who, under the pretext of acting under the protection of our flag, raised all the taxes they could. Our protectorate cost us a lot and we got no advantage from it whatsoever.

Then it was after some time we saw some changes. We owe them to the intervention of the civilian element in our colonies. Mr. Thomson, previous Prefect of the Loire region, after being nominated Governor of Cochin-China, started the process. He believed he could, by using all his energy, improve the fate of our settlers. Nonetheless, he did not reach the goal he aimed at, because he could not overcome the differences between the various interest groups. The main problem was that he rushed things. In June 1884, he forced the King to sign a treaty under which we relieved him (the King) of all administrative, judicial, financial and commercial reforms which would allow the existence of our protectorate. In a word, the French administration replaced the Cambodian administration while keeping the main Cambodian civil servants at their posts.

Unfortunately, the discontent of the King, on whom we had put some pressure and the unwillingness of the Mandarins to accept the new administrative modes soon gave rise to an insurrection which was to last two years.

Only in 1886 Mr. Piquet, previous Director of the Department of the Interior in Saigon, having been appointed Resident of France in Cambodia put an end to the confusion which had taken place. With the support of the King, he convinced the Cambodian people that France did not wish to conquer the kingdom but simply exercise the rights given to them by the protectorate status of their country. Thanks to these wise promises the country immediately regained some calm! Nevertheless, it is sad to say that, at the time, Mr. Piquet did not have the full support of the Governor of Cochin-China whose administrative point of view was different.

It was then some time later, when Mr. de Lanessan, Deputy of the Seine, was entrusted with administration in Indochina, that our situation in Cambodia was definitely strongly established.

In agreement with Mr. Piquet, Mr. de Lanessan who was to become Governor General of Indochina shortly afterwards, convinced the King of the benefits he could obtain once the reforms we (the French) were offering were put in place. Then the King revoked the ordinance relative to the private ownership of property which, until then, had been in place in Cambodia. I have already mentioned this ordinance. Finally, with a second ordinance it was decided that Mr. Piquet, Resident of the Republic of France, would be nominated Honorary President of the Cabinet and would be in charge of the reorganization of the finances of the kingdom.

Such were the bases of the new treaty, so to speak, a treaty which was enforced when Mr. de Lanessan took up his post as Governor.

Since then, Cambodia has really flourished; the King, rid of all his worries, got a "civil list" (salary) of about 360.000 piastres; the taxes come in without difficulty. I will explain the results obtained by this new administration by saying that, since 1890, Cambodia's budget doubled. We have already done a lot, I am pleased to acknowledge that, but there is still a long career ahead for our people in power for them to benefit from the huge resources which our settlers may find in a brand new country like Cambodia.

The right to own property was created for the city of Phnôm-Penh; trading houses were set up as well. But it was not enough. This is why I will finish with a requirement which will certainly soon materialize. It is to see this same right to own property put in place in the interior of the country. (In short, foreigners could buy and sell land). Cambodia is a big country and its riversides are hardly populated. Therefore our settlers should be allowed to exploit not only the sides of the rivers but also all the resources inland by making their right of becoming land owners more accessible so that they can settle on vast pieces of land. Obviously, it will take a long time but one has to start somewhere. Our beautiful France itself, once upon a time, was an uncultivated country. The monks started to clear the land, and it took several centuries before it became fertile and productive.

Let us hope that it will be the same for the whole of Indochina and particularly for Cambodia. Let us hope that after having been one of the most illustrious kingdoms of ancient times, it will rise from its ashes and will regain its importance under the powerful wing of our Republic which can do everything because it is grand, strong and because its duty is to defend the honor of France, even beyond the Oceans.

ADDITIONAL PHOTOGRAPHS

A Dancer of the King in Phnom Penh

PNOMPENH - Nº 17- La facade du Palais du Roi
au sud de la porte d'entrée principale

The facade of the King's Palace south of the main entrance door

PNOMPENH - N° 18 - Tribune de gala et facade du Palais du Roi au nord de la porte d'entrée

Pnompenh 18 – Official Pavillon of the Palace of the King north of the entrance

Pnom Penh 20 – The inauguration festivities of the Royal Pagoda
(Inside court)

Pnom Penh 21 – Palace interior – the living quarters
of His Majesty Norodom I

CAMBODGE: Pnom-Penh - Palais royal.

Photograph 8 – Boulevard in front of the Royal Palace

PNOMPENH - N° 16 - Entrée du Palais de S. M. Norodom 1er

Pnom Penh 16 – Entrance to the Palace of His Majesty Norodom I

Pnom Penh 6 – The most beautiful elephant belonging to His Majesty Norodom

Kompong Phe (opposite the Royal Palace) - Phnom Penh

Pnom Penh 15 – Boat – bathhouse for the wives of His Majesty Norodom I

Pnom Penh 5 – Market Bridge

Pnom Penh 10 – The Customs
(This building exists today.)

Pnom Penh 8 – Female Annamites and coconuts

Pnom Penh 22 – A country house (suburbs)

Pnom Penh 11 – Residence Superieur Headquarters
(Still exists.)

PNOMPENH - N° 13 - Hôpital mixte (vue d'ensemble)

Pnom Penh 13 – Mixed Hospital – view of the exterior

PNOMPENH - N° 6 - Entrée de l'Hopital

Pnom Penh 6- Hospital entrance

PNOMPENH - Nº 15
Le Directeuret les professeurs de l'Ecole Cambodgienne

Pnom Penh 15 – The director and professors of the
Cambodian School

PNOMPENH - Nº 14
Grope des enfants l'Ecole Cambodgienne

Pnom Penh 14 – Group of children at the Ecole Cambodgienne

Pnom Penh 10 – Group of Malayans on the Boulevard de la Pyramide

Pnom Penh 20 – Back to back harness of a Cambodian horse

Pnom Penh 13 – Annamite wet nurse on the dock

Pnom Penh 8 – Weapons and baggage of militia descending from Laos

Pnom Penh 1- Annamite woman

Pnom Penh 19 – Indian and Chinese Compradores

Pnom Penh 23 – Cambodian village (suburbs)

Pnom Penh 24 – Indigenous woman
supervising agricultural growth in the suburbs

Pnom Penh 4 – Regatta at the Water Festival

Pnom Penh 14 – Cambodian infantry

Pnom Penh 11 – Cargo barque navigating under sail

Pnom Penh 3 – Canoe with 20 paddlers on the Tonle Sap

Pnom Penh 21 – Drawbridge (suburbs)

1684 Kampong Cham, Women winnowing rice.

CAMBODGE: Pnom-Penh - Palais royal.

The Royal Palace looking south

PNOM-PENH - Le Pont de Takéo

Takeo Bridge between what is now
Sihanouk and Suramarith Boulevards

Série du Cambodge. — Prince Cambodgien.

A Young Cambodian Prince

Jeune Danseuse Cambodgienne

A Young Cambodian Dancer

Collection Poujade de Ladeveze

30. CAMBODGE - Environs de Pnom-Penh
Décorticage du riz dans une Ferme

Winnowing rice on a farm

Administration Headquarters at Phnom Penh

BIBLIOGRAPHY

Claude et Cie. French Government, *Annuaire Illustre du Cambodge*, Librairies Editeur, Saigon, 1904.

"Exposition coloniale organisee par la chambre de commerce a l'Exposition universelle de Lyon en 1894", Pila Chambre de commerce et d'industrie. The article entitled "Le Cambodge" runs from page 162 through page 192 and adds at the end the author is identified by the two initials "C. C." At the back of the book under the heading of "Composition de l'administration et du personnel" under the subheading of "Palais de l'indochine," under IV, "Cambodge" the text is "Commissaire. M. B. Marrot, negociant a Phnom- Penh." On page 270, under the heading "Collaborateurs Medailles D'or," on page 271, Marrot (B.), Commissaire du Cambodge was identified as receiving a gold medal.

Garnler, Francis. "Voyages d'exploration en Indochine," April 1869, quoted in C.M. Andrew and A. S. Kayna-Forstner, "Center and Periphery in the Making of the Second French Colonial Empire, 1815-1920," Journal of Imperial and Commonwealth History.

Muller, Gregor. *Colonial Cambodia's 'Bad Frenchmen': The rise of French rule and the life of Thomas Caraman, 1840-47.* (Routledge Studies in the Modern History of Asia) Routledge, 2006. Now available in French.

Osborne, Milton. *Phnom Penh: A Cultural History*, Oxford University Press, New York, 2008.

Vidal, Florence (trans.) *La Fete S'invite.* Lyon, 1894.

ACKNOWLEDGEMENTS

Marie-Helene and I would like to thank the following individuals and institutions. Foremost among the individuals are Jim Mizerski whose knowledge about and dedication to surfacing new and unrecognized material on Cambodian history and photography cannot be matched. We have had the good fortune of working with him on a number of books and in each case his sound judgment and editorial skills are unmatched. I should also like to thank Lorraine Maxwell with whom I have worked on numerous projects over two decades and her memory, editorial skills and friendship have been never properly recognized. Gregor Muller, authority on French business man Thomas Caraman, has provided thoughtful guidance for this work and others. Thanks also go to Kent Davis, the head of DatAsia Press, whose publications on Cambodia have set an example for excellence never achieved by any other publisher. My thanks also to Artsiom Yatsevich of DigitalHeavenStudio@gmail.com whose work in photo restoration and enhancement sets the standard for the publishing world.

In terms of institutions, Departement de l'Orientation et de la Recherche Bibliographique Bibliotheque Nationale de France has been extraordinarily thorough and prompt in terms of responding to my many questions directed at the Bibliotheque Nationale over many years. The Bibliotheque Nationale sets the standard for surfacing obscure information about important subjects and all of us who do research on Indochina have them to thank for their assistance. I should also recognize that the staff and technicians of the Wellesley Free Library in Wellesley, Massachusetts deserve heartfelt thanks for their endless work at locating rare books on Cambodia, Vietnam and Kouang-Tcheou-Wan (China) over a period of many years.

Exotic Visions of French Indochina

Unknown Temples of Ancient Cambodia.
ISBN: 978-1-934431-90-0

A Romance of Colonial Cambodia.
ISBN 978-1-934431-94-8

Origins of the Cambodian Ballet.
ISBN: 978-1934431-12-2

A Romance of Colonial Cambodia.
ISBN: 978-1-934431-16-0

Exotic Visions of French Indochina

An American in 1920s Indochina.
978-1-934431-82-5

A Sensual Novel of East and West.
978-1-934431-88-7

Fantastic Folktales From Ages Past.
ISBN 978-1-934431-21-4

Analysis of Cambodian Dance
97-8-1934431-29-0

Exotic Visions of French Indochina

Picture Postcards of Cambodia: 1900-1950
ISBN-13: 978-9744801197

Cambodian Shop Signs
ISBN-13: 978-1934431931

A Travel Journal of the Cambodian Mekong
ISBN-13: 978-1934431870

Notes on Cambodia's Past
ISBN-13: 978-1934431627

A Rare Artistic Tribute to French Indochina in 1923

French artist André Joyeux published this visually stunning homage to Indochina in memory of his friend, Pierre Rey, who was killed in action during WWI. Joyeux brought each of Rey's 33 French sonnets to life in his series of vibrant watercolors.

This full color, modern edition includes his paintings, the first English translation of the original foreword by Albert Saurraut, former Governor-General of French Indochina, and a biographical profile of both artists in a preface by researcher Joel Montague.

ISBN: 978-1934431917

www.ingramcontent.com/pod-product-compliance
Lightning Source LLC
Chambersburg PA
CBHW081737100526
44591CB00016B/2653